It is Time...

...to step out in your calling

Michael Marcel

UK Wells

Endorsements

"For the past 10 years prophets have been prophesying that the 21st century Church will look entirely different from what we have seen up to now. We have yet to experience this. In this book Michael raises questions and offers some solutions for the future reformation of the church; including the need for people to turn their faces and gifts towards our society so that it can be changed. You will find this book a worthwhile challenge."

Dr Sharon Stone, founder and Apostle of Christian International Europe.

- - -

"Michael Marcel presents in his new book various viewpoints from history, theology and other references that express the burning passion of his heart to see the real Church (the People) and not the building become the Church in the workplace, marketplace, home etc. He wishes to see the desires of God's heart come to pass, to have the word become flesh and move into the neighbourhood. I believe it will make very educating and enlightening reading for those who are desperate to do more for God."

Dr Sola Fola-Alade, Senior Pastor Trinity Chapel, Stratford, London, author of "Discover Your Hidden Treasures" and "So Who Do You really think You Are?"

"Michael's book makes a great read. It is informative as it casts a new light on aspects of church history. It is also a challenge to the status quo of church life as we so often experience it in Western Christianity. The reader will hear a call throughout the book for the reshaping of church, but, I anticipate the most powerful element in the book is vision of the release of the gifts that are within the body of Christ. To the reader I say: The pages you will read will invite you to enter a journey of both discovering the call of God and the release of that call. If the body of Christ is released the church will be reformed. This book will make a significant contribution toward that process."

Martin Scott, author of "Embracing Tomorrow", "Gaining Ground" and "Impacting the City".

- - -

"Michael has written with conviction, touching on poignant issues that call for the attention of a progressive Body of Christ. His in-depth analysis of the historical journey of the Church particularly in Britain makes "It Is Time... to step out in your calling" a must read; so also are his well argued reasons for some faulty foundations in the Church today. This is one book that has to be read with an open mind and with due consideration of the word of scripture that cautions on knowing in part and prophesying in part (1 Cor 13:9). I highly recommend his book."

Obii Pax-Harry, Pastor, Author of "Prophetic Engagement-The Issachar Mandate" and "Breaking Bonds of Wickedness in The Last Days".

Contents

It is Time...

Introduction

To begin with let me tell you something about myself and why I am writing this book.

My name is Michael; I was brought up in London and I first qualified as a Chartered Accountant and then in my early thirties I did an MBA. I came to the Lord in 1987 at the relatively mature age of 37. Since that time I have remained in the same family of churches, serving in various areas. During the first few years I was serving in my own strength, but the Lord set me on fire in 1994, during a visit to the Toronto Airport Christian Fellowship.

In 2002 I wrote a booklet called 'God's Heart for a Dying Land' in which I wrote on the state of the nation, our spiritual heritage, the need for unity and for the Body of Christ to pray and step out. My heart then and now is for the United Kingdom and I can see clearly the danger it is in. It is five years since I wrote that booklet; but sadly we seem to be further from God than we have ever been and I feel like I have to cry out again for the Body of Christ to arise!

For the last few years I have been looking at the state of England and I have asked myself many times, 'Why are we in this situation?' There seemed to be a contradiction in that I knew what the Bible said about the Body of Christ and so I could not understand, if that was true, why the nation was in such a dreadful state. Even with a decline in the number of Christians I thought that if all were walking in their 'calling', walking in what God had called them to do, then the Church and the nation would be in a healthy condition. Clearly, even a casual observer would realise that neither the Church nor society is in a healthy state, so it followed that Christians were not walking in their 'calling,' but why?

I have spent several years wondering what was wrong with my equation; the church I was in seemed to be a pretty good place to be and I knew a number of strong Christians from various churches, and yet I knew few people who were really making a difference in society and very few who were living out the words of the Great Commission in Mark 16:15-18:

"Go into all the world and preach the good news to all creation. Whoever believes and is baptised will be saved, but whoever does not believe will be condemned. And these signs will accompany those who believe: In my name they will drive out demons; they will speak in new tongues; they will pick up snakes with their hands; and when they drink deadly poison, it will not hurt them at all; they will place their hands on sick people, and they will get well."

My life verse is Ephesians 4:12:

'to prepare God's people for works of service, so that the body of Christ may be built up.'

The New King James and the New American Standard talk about 'equipping the saints.' This verse inspired me to read books and to go around the world so that I might be equipped to fulfil the calling on my life, but what I couldn't understand was why I was not receiving this in my church.

Finally I began to understand what was wrong; I had been looking at the problem from the wrong perspective; taking for granted that everything I had been taught about the Church and about the physical church that surrounded me; was truth. I then read two books by Frank Viola, 'Rethinking the Wineskin' and 'Pagan Christianity' and these helped me to find answers as to why the Church has not impacted society the way it should.

For many years it has been my burning passion to fulfil the calling that my God has chosen for me and to see every person in the Body of Christ doing the same thing. So although I do not consider myself a theologian or teacher I decided to try and explain through a book why so many are not stepping out in their calling and by doing this I pray that some will have their eyes opened and will be able to move forward into their destiny.

In this book I hope to show how the Church has changed over time, from its first days in the Book of Acts, up to today; when it has become incapable, in many cases, of being able to fulfil Ephesians 4:12. I believe that God is calling for a new wineskin to achieve this. I try to show what has prevented us from fulfilling God's plan for us, and how we can all change and step out in our calling, so that society and the nation can be changed. The situation may look bleak at the moment, but the future can be redeemed.

Several of the points I make deserve whole books to be written on them, indeed many have been, but my intention is to show aspects of church history in a short and concise way. Please understand that writing in this manner means that I have had to leave out a mass of information that some of you may be interested in. Please get hold of the books listed in the bibliography and there you can read the subjects in much greater detail. It is very important to look at the history of the Church to give us an understanding of how we got to this place; this will then help to show us what needs to change so that we can move forward.

CHAPTER 1

The state of our Nation

I have stated above that the nation is in a 'dreadful state'. I try to back up that statement in this chapter.

'Arise, shine, for your light has come, and the glory of the LORD rises upon you. See, darkness covers the earth and thick darkness is over the peoples, but the LORD rises upon you and his glory appears over you'. (Isaiah 60:1-2)

You will notice from the above passage that one had to see the darkness that covered the earth and the peoples, before the glory came, so I am going to begin by describing some of the 'darkness' that besets our society. As time goes by there is a danger that we just get used to these 'evils' and accept them as the norm, so although this section is quite long, I feel it important to list them in a certain amount of detail.

The facts that I quote below are to do with the United Kingdom but if you are from another nation I am sure that several of these conditions will exist in your country also. Please understand that it is not my intention to offend anyone through what I have written.

Abortion

In 1968 there were a total of 23,641 abortions performed in England and Wales. A peak of 187,402 abortions was reached in 1998, but the figures have dropped only to 186,400 in 2005. Close to 6.7 million abortions have been performed in England and Wales in the forty years since the 1967 Abortion Act was passed. Figures for Scotland show a similar steady rise from a total of 1,544 abortions in 1968 to 12,603 in 2005. This is the highest level ever. (These are all from ONS government statistics).

At the time of writing we have has just passed the 40th anniversary of the Abortion Act (27th October 2007). The Parliamentary Science and Technology Committee have also just reported on scientific developments relating to the Abortion Act of 1967. In this report they concluded that:

a) There is no scientific basis to reduce the 24 week upper limit for abortion.

b) The requirement for two doctors' signatures before an abortion can be carried out should be removed.

c) Nurses and midwives should be allowed to carry out early abortions.

d) Foetal pain is not relevant to the question of abortion law.

Two members of the committee wrote a report disagreeing with their 9 colleagues. The committee considered the evidence from 5 pro-life groups compared with 13 pro-abortion groups. Despite the many voices that are saying that the numbers of abortions each year are 'appalling'; this influential committee appears determined to try to make abortion even easier.

Alcohol

According to a report from Alcohol Concern, the amount of alcohol consumed by girls aged 11-13 has increased by 82.6% from 2000-2006; while for boys the amount has gone up by 43.4% during the same period. This means that alcohol consumption has more than doubled for boys and girls since 1994. The report says, 'Binge drinking by children can have serious consequences for brain function, significantly raises the risk of alcohol dependency in later life and diminishes their life chances.'

An article in the Daily Express on March 12th 2007 says that, 'the cost of yobbish behaviour has more than doubled in Britain since the introduction of 24 hour drinking according to research. Damage caused by drunken louts reached a staggering £4.3 billion last year, with one in five businesses across the country affected.

Church

As we are all aware, church attendance has been in severe decline over recent years. Statistics from the organisation 'Christian Research' in their 2005 English Church Census show that the number of people who attended church on Sunday has declined from 5.44 million in 1979 to 3.17 (6.3%) million in 2005, a drop of 42% in 26 years. The decline has slowed down recently, mainly due to the number of Africans that are now in our churches. In London 44% of church goers are black. From 1998-2005 the Catholic Church has declined 27% in Sunday attendance, the Methodists 24% and the Church of England 11%, however the Pentecostal churches have seen an increase of 34% in the same period.

Cloning

The Draft Human Tissue and Embryology Bill was published in June 2007. Points highlighted by the Lawyer's Christian Fellowship are:

1)   It is proposed that the Reproductive Cloning Act 2001, which banned reproductive cloning, be repealed and replaced by something far less clear cut (clause 16, para 15.5);

2)   The Bill will allow scientists to create any variety of animal-human hybrid embryos for research purposes (clause 17);

3)   It is proposed that non-profit making bodies be allowed to advertise in order to facilitate surrogacy arrangements (clause 66).

The reason the Prime Minister gave was to keep us in the forefront of research. We, as a nation, have legalised cloning so that we can make money.

Drugs

It is obvious that drug use is increasing in our society at a substantial rate, and there are many problems that come from this, such as the spread of AIDS and drug-related crime. The talk now is to legalise cannabis and have drug cafes as they have in Holland. A Government statistic that has really impacted me is that three times as many 11 to 13 year-olds have taken drugs during 2003 compared with 1998.

Education

The education of our children is in the hands of teachers who undoubtedly want the best for them, but many have liberal mindsets and they are in danger of damaging those they want to help. The greatest danger in schools today is the teaching that truth is relative and there is no such thing as 'right and wrong'. Another major problem is that children as young as six are being taught about homosexuality with drawings and descriptions in their text books. We must be aware of what our children are being taught. I urge you to check on what the schools are teaching your children.

Euthanasia

This is an evil that is creeping up on us. Holland has already legalised euthanasia, and people are beginning to make it an issue in the courts of this country. Diane Pretty took the issue to the Court of Human Rights to ask for the right to have her husband help her to die. On this occasion, the Court of Human Rights ruled against her, but clearly this is an issue that is not going to go away.

CARE says; 'Christians believe that humans are created by God in His image (Genesis 1:26-27, Genesis 9:5-6) and since the Bible promotes the sanctity of life (Exodus 20:13, 23:7) human life is God's gift to us. We are not the owners, but rather the stewards of it. Christians also believe that as a society we have a moral obligation and social responsibility to care for all people with dignity and respect, especially those who are elderly, dying or disabled. The legalisation of euthanasia would result in pressure, real and/or perceived, for the vulnerable to request euthanasia, so that they are "not a burden".

'Conversely, there is a strong humanist movement to allow people to have the "right to die" and to allow individuals "patient autonomy" so that each of us can choose when it is right for us to die. Allowing euthanasia would lead to judgements being made about which lives were worth living and which were not. The danger for those who may not be considered to have worthwhile lives - the elderly, the mentally and physically disabled, long term prisoners - is all too clear.'

'The Mental Capacity Act 2005 allows doctors to remove life-sustaining treatment which includes the provision of food and water if the patient has stated by an advanced directive that they don't want to be kept alive by life-sustaining treatment when they are no longer compos mentis. This is arguably a form of euthanasia.'

Family breakdown

The Office of National Statistics in 2005 showed that the United Kingdom had the third highest divorce rate in Europe, around 167,000; they also show that in 2006 24% of children lived in a one-parent family, more than three times the proportion in 1972. Where there are children, half of cohabiting couples part within ten years, compared to just one in eight of married parents.

This trend towards fewer people getting married is resulting in more and more problems for society. A 2007 Unicef report states that Britain came bottom of 21 countries with regard to children's well-being, particularly in relationships, behaviour and self-esteem. This is largely due to the high number of single parent families and step families which result in a greater risk of children dropping out of school, leaving school early, poorer health, low skills and low pay. The report also says that Britain has high rates of obesity, drunkenness, bullying, early sexual intercourse, cannabis-taking and teenage pregnancy.

CARE quotes many research sources in their excellent booklet 'For Better or For Worse,' when it discusses this point: 'There is overwhelming evidence that the break-up of partnerships or marriages is damaging to children; the resulting instability means that children are more likely to suffer from poor performance in school and a lack of concentration and are more anxious and attention seeking when young. They are more likely to fall ill, to have behavioural problems, to fall prey to solvent, drug and alcohol abuse and to come before the criminal courts.'

A child, particularly a boy growing up in a home without a father, is at a disadvantage. Again I quote from 'For Better or For Worse.' 'Absent fatherhood can lead to greater conflict between mothers and their sons…the aggressive behaviour of boys tends to escalate.' Boys need to have a healthy male role model to identify with, so that their masculinity can mature the way God intended. A stable family environment is vital to the wellbeing of society.

In March 2002, at a Conference in Westminster, Rev. Dr. Clifford Hill made a statement that he then released to the Press (see The Daily Telegraph 11/3/02). Dr Hill runs a Christian research organization called The Family Matters Institute. In 1998 they did research into the cost of marriage breakdown. Jack Straw, the then Home Secretary, came to hear a presentation where they revealed the cost to be a staggering £15 billion. Evidently Jack Straw was impressed and the Government issued a Green Paper that proposed supporting the institution of the family. However, this Paper never became law, because people in the Cabinet, who are against the family, had it thrown out.

The New Labour Government of the last 10 years has been noticeably against the institution of the traditional family and due to the strength of the homosexual lobby at the centre of government, alternative lifestyles have been promoted to the disadvantage of families.

Gambling

Gambling is a major blot on the landscape of Britain. Over the last few years, since the introduction of the Lottery and on-line gambling, there has been a tremendous increase in gambling. A May 2007 survey for the Gambling Commission shows that 8.4% of the adult population participated in remote gambling in the previous month, an increase of 6% on the previous year. The Government seems to have a great interest in trying to get us to gamble, fortunately their plans for eight mega Casinos in the UK have been thwarted for the moment, but they still gave the go ahead for more casinos recently. The BMA produced a report in January 2007, worried about the rise in addiction that will come from the Government's new Gambling Act. The industry is estimated to be worth £40bn a year and addicts are estimated at 350,000, and this figure can only increase.

Homosexuality

At this point I would like to mention that I make comments on homosexuality quite frequently in this chapter. The reason for this is that the homosexual lobby has recently become very powerful in Government, and through their influence they are trying to change the laws of this country. Their agenda is no longer to just get people to accept them into society; it is now to try to change the law so that no one can criticise them and to get our children taught that homosexuality is a good life style. Through their political agenda the homosexual lobby is coming into direct conflict with Christians and it appears from their actions that this is a deliberate policy.

As Christians we need to reach out to those living a lifestyle of homosexuality in love and not judgment, to try to bring them to knowledge of God and inner healing. However, the political arm of homosexuality is attacking our Christian way of life and this must be resisted. It is estimated that around 2% of our population are living a lifestyle of homosexuality and lesbianism, and yet the way we are bombarded through the television and media, one would have thought the figure was around 50%. The power that they have gained through

Government, the Arts and Media is way out of proportion to their numbers.

On the radio and television anyone who does not accept homosexuality is deemed to be homophobic and the term is used in a very derogatory way. To be anti-homosexual is deemed to be not 'politically correct.' Whether it is about homosexuality or anything else we must stop being 'politically correct' and stand up and be 'biblically correct.'

The Bible speaks out against homosexuality, (Leviticus 18:22, also note Romans 1:27 and 1 Corinthians 6:9). However, we must remember that the Bible speaks out against adultery as well. Marriage between a man and a woman is the biblical model and the only acceptable one. There is a good reason why the Bible advocates marriage. Every child needs to be fed by male and female love, so that he can grow according to God's plan. Homosexuality often comes about because a child has an abusive, absent or weak father or a dominating mother, so they grow up with no good male role model. Because of this many children are growing up with a warped sense of the 'father's love' and 'masculinity', and so some reach out towards the first male love that they find, in order to fulfil their need for male affirmation. Generally speaking homosexuality comes out of rejection, loneliness and the need for love; as Christians we know that God loves them and we need to try to bring the Lord's love and healing to the brokenness inside them.

Islam

According to the BBC, Islam is the fastest growing religion in the world and there are 2 million Muslims in this country. Reliable statistics do not support the first contention and I am not sure about the second. However, many there are their growth is mainly due to the fact that the majority of asylum seekers have been from Islamic nations, and there has been considerable immigration from Asia.

A subject of great concern is the avowed intention of some of the Muslim leaders to make Britain an Islamic State and the leading Islamic Nation in

Europe. Obviously the majority of Muslims in Britain are peace-loving people, but many of the Mullahs are fundamentalists and are preaching extreme doctrine, especially to the young. There is a strong Islamist agenda in the UK, they keep claiming new rights within our society and in some areas Sharia Law is being practised. They are often commenting on the way Muslims are treated around the world and yet you never hear that the penalty for a Muslim turning to Christianity in some Islamic countries is death. I have tried to get the BBC to tell something of the truth about the Islamic agenda apart from the sanitised version they give, but to no effect.

Lawlessness

The prison population stood at 80,316 on March 30th 2007; the prisons are at capacity, reflecting the violence of our society. The Government has had some success in bringing down the crime statistics, but we all know it is still a big problem in our society. The recent spate of knife killings by teenagers in London is yet another sign of the deep rooted problems in our society.

Media

It is a fairly obvious statement, but the media has enormous power over people's views and attitudes and it is largely non-Christian.

I find that there is very little left on television that I can watch. There is nearly always a warning against comedy or drama programmes, about violence, language or sexual content. I cannot remember the last new programme that did not bring in adultery somewhere in the story. Homosexuality is now creeping into children's programmes (Dr Who and Torchwood), let alone adult slots. The creator of 'Torchwood', Russell T Davies said:

'Without making it political or dull, this is going to be a very bisexual programme. I want to knock down the barriers so we can't define which of the characters is gay. We need to start mixing things up, rather than thinking, 'This is a gay character and he'll only ever go off with men.'

13

There are now pornographic films on before 11.00pm and the content of most 'soaps' make them unsuitable viewing.

I listen to quite a lot of Radio while driving and over the last few months I have e-mailed the BBC, complaining about their bias. The way the establishment and Christianity is mocked and belittled is quite frightening. However, the favourable attitude towards Muslims is in marked contrast.

It was reported in the newspapers in October 2006 that there was a secret meeting in London, which was hosted by veteran broadcaster Sue Lawley, where BBC executives admitted the corporation is dominated by homosexuals and people from ethnic minorities, deliberately promotes multiculturalism, is anti-American, anti-countryside and more sensitive to the feelings of Muslims than Christians. One veteran BBC executive said: 'There was widespread acknowledgement that we may have gone too far in the direction of political correctness. Unfortunately, much of it is so deeply embedded in the BBC's culture, that it is very hard to change it.' What an incredible situation, that an organisation that was so respected around the world for its fair reporting has become as biased as a Soviet Government television station.

At the same time Christian radio is under attack. In November 2001 Colin R Nicholl wrote an article in 'The Spectator'. I set out below some quotes from this article: 'Premier Radio has been given a "Yellow Card" by the Radio Authority. This means that if the station does not mend its ways it could lose its licence'. 'The Radio Authority's Quarterly Complaints Bulletin (July-September 2001), had 14 programming complaints and one advertising complaint lodged against it.... every single complaint about Premier Radio was from the "Mysticism and Occultism Federation"'.

'The Federation has five part-time unpaid volunteers who monitor the media, particularly Christian media.' 'And the Radio Authority has even pledged to join the occultists in monitoring closely Premier Radio's output.'

Another complaint was 'An evangelical minister, Dr Michael Youssef, in a sermon on the lame man at Bethesda, suggested that mainline churches were following a PC agenda and accommodating to secular culture instead of trusting in Jesus alone, "the true redeemer" the true Saviour, the only one who can make them whole'. He insisted that the only cure for our society was following the word of Jesus Christ. In addition, Dr Youssef expressed his conviction that it was "crazy" to claim that one can be a "practising homosexual" and a "good Christian" at the same time, in view of Paul's teaching in 1 Romans. Concurring with the occultists' complaint that these comments were "offensive", the Radio Authority judged that they "denigrated the beliefs of other people" and thus contravened the Programme Code'.

'..is it now the case that only those Christians who interpret the Bible as permitting homosexual practice can air their views on radio?'

'Another well-known evangelical preacher, Dr Charles Swindoll, warned Christians of the dangers of "dabbling in the occult" and advised them to destroy any occult materials in their possession. In advocating this, Dr Swindoll was merely reiterating the counsel of Acts 19:19. However, in a rather fascinating PC judgement, the Radio Authority asserted that "divination" was a part of some religious belief systems, and that Swindoll's homily was tantamount to denigration of others' beliefs. This ruling raises a number of questions: since Satanists worship Satan, is it similarly offensive to portray Satan in negative terms?'

'..Stations must be vigilant not to abuse any religious beliefs whatsoever, regardless of whether the audience at whom the service was aimed might themselves be offended or not.'

'The authority is making an ass of the broadcasting legislation with its PC judgements which fundamentally undermine the freedom of religious expression for Christians.'

'We can only hope that the Radio Authority turns back from this petty madness before it goes any further.'

We should be thankful that there are organisations such as the Centre for Justice and Liberty that are fighting for freedom for Christian Broadcasting.

Occult

Through the hunger of people to experience something supernatural, there has been a massive increase in interest in the occult over the last 20 years. Again, like homosexuality, the occult has been given the aura of normality by the media, through TV shows like Buffy the Vampire Slayer, Charmed, Sabrina the Teenage Witch and Supernatural. These programmes are targeting young people from four to twenty, as are games such as Pokemon, Tarot Cards and Dungeons and Dragons. These are all entry-level tools that introduce young people to witchcraft, sorcery etc.

Deuteronomy 18:10-12 makes God's view very clear on such matters. Cindy Jacobs has published an excellent book called 'Deliver Us from Evil', which explains all forms of the occult and gives warning signs and advice to parents. She began to write the book after she had visited a few bookshops and saw row upon row of occult books. Look for yourself. I found an occult book in the Christianity section of one multiple bookstore. Please do not underestimate this problem. Membership of the occult is growing and one of the main targets of occultist groups are pastors. They pray against the health and marriages of pastors, and so we must protect our leaders through our own prayers. I know a vicar who was praying around his parish when he saw a man also praying. He went up to the man and asked him what he was praying about, and he replied that he was an occultist who was praying against the church leaders in the area.

Paedophilia

Everybody must have noticed the increased incidence of paedophilia. In June 2007 the BBC reported *'Jim Gamble, of the Child Exploitation and Online*

Protection Centre (CEOP), said some offenders who viewed child porn could be given a police caution.' Paedophilia is so widespread that there are not enough prison places to deal with them. The BBC further reported *'Research by the National Society for the Prevention of Cruelty to Children (NSPCC) found that 16% of women and 7% of men claimed to have been sexually abused involving physical contact before the age of 12. That suggests that one in nine pre-teenage children has suffered abuse.'*

Persecution

Persecution and attacks on the principle of 'freedom of speech' is becoming more and more prevalent. In April 2002 a Muslim chaplain, with the support of several student bodies, put together a paper entitled `Faiths Together on Campus', outlining the need to have organisations, primarily from the evangelical camp, banned from proselytising on any UK based campus.

I have mentioned above that the 'Mysticism and Occult Federation' is trying to stop biblical truths being spoken on the radio. In April 2002 The Mail on Sunday reported that a 69 year-old man was preaching in the street the biblical truths about immorality. He had mud and water thrown at him by homosexual activists and the courts fined him, because they decided that the sign he carried (Stop immorality, stop homosexuality, stop lesbianism) provoked violence. One may think that this man acted a little unwisely, but the point is, and I quote the newspaper 'The Law of England is supposed to punish actions, not thoughts'.

In November 2003 the Bishop of Chester was investigated by the police after he told his local newspaper about research showing that some homosexuals re-orientated to heterosexuality. The Crown Prosecution Service decided not to prosecute.

A Glasgow fireman was demoted for refusing to take part in a 'gay pride' march. The Christian Institute helped him get reinstated.

Stephen Green of Christian Voice handed out Christian leaflets at a gay rally;
he was arrested and committed for trial but the CPS dropped the case. A police
spokesman confirmed that Mr Green had not behaved aggressively, violently
or caused an obstruction but that he had been arrested because "the leaflet
contained Biblical quotes about homosexuality."

A couple telephoned their Council to complain about its gay rights policy; the
Council asked the police to intervene. Two police officers visited the couple
to educate them about their Christian beliefs on homosexuality. In 2007 the
Christian Institute forced the Council and the police to back down.

On June 29th 2006 the Gay Police Association placed an advertisement in the
Independent newspaper entitled 'in the name of the father' with a picture of a
red Bible next to a pool of blood. It said 'in the last 12 months the Gay Police
Association has recorded a 74% increase in homophobic incidents, where the
sole or primary motivating factor was the religious belief of the perpetrator.'
Colin Hart of the Christian Institute summed up the feelings of most Christians
over this advertisement when he said 'This virulently anti-Christian advert
was placed by the Gay Police Association (GPA). The grossly offensive and
wholly unsubstantiated message of the ad is that Bible believers are causing
an explosion of violent attacks on homosexuals, and that the bloodshed has to
stop. The advert plainly implies that Christians are responsible for violence
against homosexuals. But violence or abusive behaviour towards any person
– homosexual or otherwise - is totally incompatible with the Christian faith.
A violent person cannot be a Bible-believing Christian. In my view the advert
stereotypes Christians as violent and hateful people. I am concerned because the
Police are there to protect my liberty, yet an officially recognised Police group
is parodying Bible-believers as violent thugs.'

The Police have a large number of homosexuals in their ranks and four of the
examples above clearly show that they are prepared to act against Christians
who disagree with the lifestyle of homosexuals. This is a very worrying
situation with freedom of conscience and freedom of speech coming under

attack from the very people who are meant to protect us. The CPS refused to prosecute the GPA and although the Advertising Standards Authority held that they had breached the Advertising Code of Conduct on three counts; decency, truthfulness and substantiation; its only sanction was that the GPA were told not to use the advertisement (which was the most complained about advertisement in 2006) again.

A Magistrate, Andrew McClintock, found himself compelled to resign from a Family Panel when he declared he would be unable to recommend children to be fostered or adopted into a same-sex household. The Lawyers Christian Fellowship reported that 'Mr McClintock was not asking for a change in the law, rather he was requesting that his religious conscience should be accommodated, and that he should be "screened" from cases which might require him to adopt children in to same-sex households.' He had his case heard by a Tribunal which reported its findings on February 28th 2007; LCF reported that 'Mr McClintock has lost his case to have his freedom of conscience recognised when practising as a Justice of the Peace. He will not be able to serve on the Family Panel, even though the Tribunal recognised that "he has an unblemished record and is well regarded by fellow magistrates and by the Department of Constitutional Affairs". On October 31st 2007, Mr McClintock lost his appeal and so now he will be unable to serve on the Family Panel.

Christian unions at several Universities are under attack for not being 'inclusive'. An example is Edinburgh University; LCF reported in November 2006 'Following pressure from a group of students, Edinburgh University has banned the University Christian Union from running one of its events on University premises. Pressure is principally coming from the Gay & Lesbian Society at Edinburgh University. The banned event is a course called PURE, which presents the Biblical basis of personal relationships. The University's decision is based on its belief that PURE is in breach of its equality and diversity policy because PURE claims that any sexual activity outside heterosexual marriage is not God-ordained. This incident is an attack on freedom of speech in an institution where an open exchange of views and a search after truth should be strongly upheld. In this instance the CU is being denied freedom of expression because what they say and believe is uncomfortable for some groups in the university.' Several of the Unions are taking the Universities to court to resolve the issues.

There are indications that some Councils are planning to withdraw grants from Christian Charities if they do not become 'inclusive'. LCF report on one example 'It came as a shock to Gosia Shannon, the organiser of a Family Centre for Eastern European migrants who have settled in London, when she was told last month by Haringey Council that unless the Centre agreed to renounce all expression of Christianity from the voluntary services they provided, they would lose the vital funding they received from the local authority.' The Council extended the funding until April 2006 after press coverage.

The Sexual Orientation Regulations came into force on April 30th 2007 despite intense Christian representations. The SOR's will force Christians in business to supply homosexuals; for instance a printer will be forced to print homosexual literature if asked and the owner of a bed and breakfast business will be forced to give a room to homosexuals even though he can refuse a heterosexual couple who are not married. These regulations put the rights of homosexuals above human rights. The LCF reported 'Christians object to these Regulations because they will force them to become involved in promoting or facilitating homosexual lifestyles contrary to the practice and teaching of the church down the centuries. The Regulations are widely misunderstood. Those promoting them talk about the need to eradicate prejudice against homosexuals not realising that without the necessary safeguards these Regulations are creating a new prejudice against those who want to live according to traditional Christian (and other mainstream beliefs) that teach that all sex outside heterosexual marriage is wrong. This should concern all those who believe in freedom of conscience and in the value of our Judeo-Christian heritage.'

Another potential problem is highlighted by the case of the Mathericks. This couple, who are in their sixties, have fostered 28 children through Somerset

20

County Council. They decided that they would have to give up fostering, rather than sign up to the new Equalities Promise. According to the Times newspaper, 'The couple, who are both ministers at the nonconformist South Chard Christian Church, said they had been told by officials that they would be required to discuss same-sex relationships with children as young as 11 and tell them that gay partnerships were just as acceptable as heterosexual marriages. Mr Matherick said: "I cannot preach the benefits of homosexuality when I believe it is against the word of God."' However, good sense has prevailed in this case. After a meeting on October 31st 2007 with the Social Services, it was agreed that they did not have to sign up to the new 'Equalities Promise'. It is only a matter of time before other Christians are going to have to make similar choices.

Finally, the latest (as at the time of writing) action by the homosexual lobby is to get the Government to amend the Criminal Justice and Immigration Bill to introduce an offence of inciting hatred on the grounds of sexuality. The Lawyer's Christian Fellowship says, 'We are very concerned about the effect this will have on the freedom of Christians and others to openly express their views and beliefs about sexuality. We are also convinced that such a law is unnecessary, as homosexuals are already adequately protected from abuse by the criminal law, in the same way that we all benefit from such protection.' This is currently being discussed in a Parliamentary Committee.

As I have already mentioned, I have written a lot in this chapter about homosexuality. I must re-iterate that I am not in any way against those living a homosexual lifestyle; I am making these points because the political agenda of the homosexual lobby is directly infringing our rights as Christians. Christians in Britain are going to suffer more and more persecution. We must speak out our Christian beliefs more than ever before. The Lawyers' Christian Fellowship and the Christian Institute are fighting for our rights and they deserve and need our support. When God's law comes into conflict with man's law we must live out God's law.

Politics

The public's view of politicians has been undermined tremendously over the last 20 years. This has been partly because of the lowering of morals by public figures, but also because the media takes enormous delight in bringing them down. Add to this the years of spin we have had to endure, and the result is a reduction of trust in political figures, scepticism of what truth is and an erosion of democracy. People's views of politics and politicians are at an all time low. In the 1999 election to decide upon the Welsh Assembly, 10% of the voters were against and a fraction over 10% were in favour. Almost 80% did not vote. The voting in General Elections and European Elections is falling all the time. The result is that minorities get into power and democracy suffers.

Sexual permissiveness

I do not have to say much about this as it is all around us. We all know that the sexual content on TV and films is greater than ever. An Office of National Statistics report in 2003 said that the UK has the highest rate of teenage pregnancy in Europe, 40% higher than second placed Portugal. The instances of sexually transmitted infection are growing fast. A report from the Health Protection Agency in 2006 shows that the number of new diagnoses in 2005 was 790,443; an increase of 75% since 1995 and 12% since 2005. Finally, the spread of pornography over the internet, including paedophilia, is a real problem.

If the situation is really going to change in this nation, we have to become involved. I would like to suggest that never in the history of Britain (except possibly in the 18th Century) have we sunk so low, spiritually and morally, and we Christians have allowed it to happen through our passivity and lack of interest. If we are going to protect our children we need to become far more active in making protests to government and the media; we have the government and media that we deserve. If we were all walking in the fullness of our calling in Christ then nothing could come against us and this nation would be transformed.

CHAPTER 2

What was the New Testament Church like?

I do not propose to give a long study on what the Church is or a history on
how it came about; what I want to discuss is the physical nature of the New
Testament Church so that we have a marker to compare the Church of today.
I will then go on to describe how the Church changed over the centuries so
that we can understand how we came to the Church we have today. Four if the
next five chapters describe Church history. This is very necessary because it is
important that we have a sound understanding of the past so that we can build a
bridge to the future.

Ekklesia

The Greek word used in the New Testament for Church is Ekklesia and it
is used three times in the Gospels, twice in Matthew 18:17 where Jesus is
speaking of discipline in the Church, but the first time it is used is in the famous
passage of Matthew 16:18:

*'And I tell you that you are Peter, and on this rock I will build my church, and
the gates of Hades will not overcome it.'*

We shall come across this passage again later on as it is one of the main
foundations of the theory of Papal Supremacy. Bishops of Rome in later
centuries will point to this verse as proof that Peter and his successors will lead
the Church and as Peter probably died in Rome, his successors, as leaders of
the Roman Church, are therefore the true heads of the Church worldwide. The
Bishops of Rome then began to call themselves 'Pope' and so then you had
Papal Supremacy that the Catholic Church still propounds today. Nothing I
write is to be taken as a criticism of 'Catholics', because until the 16th Century
we were all 'Catholics' as there was only one denomination in the Church in the
UK at that time.

However in Matthew 16:18 'this' does not mean the person Peter; it means the revelation of the Lordship of Jesus Christ that Peter had been expressing in verse 16. Jesus will build his Church on the faith of those people who realise that He is the Christ, the Son of the living God.

It must be clearly understood that Ekklesia never means a building; it means an assembly that can meet in many places. In the 21st Century the word 'church' immediately brings to mind a building, maybe a cathedral or a local church or chapel, but 1st Century Christians would never have looked at the word that way. In those days the word 'ekklesia' was a familiar one, as it meant any assembly that came out of a body of people. The Greek word 'ek' means 'out' and 'kalein' means 'to call'. Throughout the Greek world citizens were used to a herald calling them out to discuss public matters.

Our word 'church' has come from the term for the place where Christians gathered together. For the first few centuries Christians met almost exclusively in private homes and these were called 'Kuriou Oikos' or 'the House of the Lord'. Over time these words were shortened into words like 'Kuriake' that became 'Kirk' in Scotland and with the softening of the 'k' to a 'ch' we get 'church'.

Pentecost

The beginning of the Church came about at Pentecost. The last words that Jesus spoke in Matthew's gospel were the Great Commission and were made before His ascension. The last verses of Mark's gospel are also instructions that we should, 'Go into all the world'. The last verses of Luke and the first verses of Acts are instructions by Jesus that the disciples must wait for the coming of the Holy Spirit. The disciples had instructions of what to do, but they could not do it without the power of the Holy Spirit that came upon them at Pentecost.

In this book I have put 'the' in front of 'Holy Spirit' because we are used to mentioning Him in that way and that is the way it is written in the Bible.

However, we must remember that the Holy Spirit is not a thing, He is a person and should be described as 'Holy Spirit'; there is no such thing as 'a' or 'the' in the Greek New Testament and we do not say 'the Jesus'.

The Bible says in Acts 2:7-8:

'Utterly amazed, they asked: "Are not all these men who are speaking Galileans? Then how is it that each of us hears them in his own native language?"'

A modern day example of this is Surprise Sithole who pastors the 7,000 plus churches of Heidi Baker in Mozambique and many other countries. Pastor Surprise could only speak Portuguese but he wanted to go to a Bible School in South Africa but they insisted that he had to know English. Pastor Surprise decided that he would go for the interview anyway and during the meeting he was asked how he learned such good English; he was astonished as he thought he was speaking Portuguese, but he had been speaking English all the time.

What happened at Pentecost? Let us look at the first few chapters of Acts. The people heard the sound of a rushing mighty wind (Acts 2:2) and came to find out what was going on. They were utterly amazed (Acts 2:7) at finding the Apostles speaking in different languages. They were amazed and perplexed (Acts 2:12) at the outpouring of the Holy Spirit and after hearing the truth about Jesus, three thousand gave their lives to the Lord (Acts 2:41).

Then comes some of my favourite verses in the Bible, Acts 2:42-45:

'They devoted themselves to the apostles' teaching and to the fellowship, to the breaking of bread and to prayer. Everyone was filled with awe, and many wonders and miraculous signs were done by the apostles. All the believers were together and had everything in common. Selling their possessions and goods, they gave to anyone as he had need.'

Everyone was filled with awe at the teaching and the miraculous and as a result all the believers had everything in common. For me the atmosphere of heaven had come down to earth and we can see exactly how the Lord wants church. The people:

1) Devoted themselves to studying the Bible.
2) Devoted themselves to fellowship.
3) Had meals together.
4) Took communion together.
5) Prayed together.
6) Experienced signs and wonders pouring out.
7) Shared everything together so that nobody was in need.

Does this not sound like a wonderful church to you? This form of church is something we should all aspire to.

The growing Church would not have met all together all the time; most of their meetings were in many different homes, but they were considered one Body. Another wonderful statement is in verse 47, where the believers were 'enjoying the favour of all the people'. Can you imagine what the atmosphere must have been like? The believers must have been shining with the Holy Spirit and they must have been full of the love of the Lord to enjoy the favour of all the people. The fruit of it all was that the Lord 'added to their number daily'.

A little while later numbers had increased to five thousand men (Acts 4:4), so with women and children there were probably 10,000 believers at that time. Then later in the same chapter the description in Acts 2:44-5 is repeated. Acts 4:32-34:

'All the believers were one in heart and mind. No one claimed that any of his possessions was his own, but they shared everything they had. With great power the apostles continued to testify to the resurrection of the Lord Jesus, and much grace was upon them all. There were no needy persons among them.'

Again, what a wonderful description of Church this is. So why does Church today look so different from how it did then? After all we still have the main ingredients: the Word, the Holy Spirit and people! Some of you may say that we do not have the miraculous today and that is why the Church is so different, but that is just not true. I can tell you that virtually every miracle in the New Testament has been repeated in some part of the world over the last few years.

I know of a man who walked to freedom through four guarded doorways in a high security prison (Acts 12:6); I know a man whose angel was mistaken for him (Acts 12:15); and I also know a woman in whose ministry the food for the orphans is often multiplied (Matt 14:15-21). I know a woman whose house, after prayer, was untouched from a tornado when houses all around were devastated; and a man who prayed for nine blind children and all were instantly healed. I have seen healed several people from a deaf school and I have been used myself to heal someone from AIDS and TB. Literally thousands of blind, deaf and lame have been healed recently all over the world. One man I know has been used to raise fifteen people from the dead and I know two Englishmen who have both been used to raise someone from the dead in England, and I have spoken to the pastor of a church where one of his people was used to do the same. Make no mistake, the Lord is pouring out His Spirit very powerfully.

Services

So now let us see what the New Testament tells us about the church services they held. Firstly, what was the purpose for the people meeting together? Ephesians 4:11-16:

'It was he who gave some to be apostles, some to be prophets, some to be evangelists, and some to be pastors and teachers, to prepare God's people for works of service, so that the body of Christ may be built up until we all reach unity in the faith and in the knowledge of the Son of God and become mature, attaining to the whole measure of the fullness of Christ. Then we will no longer be infants, tossed back and forth by the waves, and blown here and

there by every wind of teaching and by the cunning and craftiness of men in their deceitful scheming. Instead, speaking the truth in love, we will in all things grow up into him who is the Head, that is, Christ. From him the whole body, joined and held together by every supporting ligament, grows and builds itself up in love, as each part does its work.'

This passage, particularly verses 11 and 12, is the main reason for my writing this book. We shall be looking at verse 11 and the first part of verse 12 later on, but in the context of the New Testament church service, the second half of verse 12 shows that its purpose was 'so that the body of Christ may be built up.' At the end of this passage it says that each person in the body needs to do his/her part so that the body can grow and build itself up in love.

This theme is repeated in Hebrews 10:24-25:

'And let us consider how we may spur one another on towards love and good deeds. Let us not give up meeting together, as some are in the habit of doing, but let us encourage one another-- and all the more as you see the Day approaching.'

And again in 1 Corinthians 14:26:

'How is it then, brethren? Whenever you come together, each of you has a psalm, has a teaching, has a tongue, has a revelation, has an interpretation. Let all things be done for edification.' (NKJV)

If one of the purposes of the Church was mutual edification, where did they meet and what did the service look like?

I have already mentioned that most of the time they met in peoples' houses. Acts 2:46 says that they met every day in the Temple courts. And Acts 5:12 says that all the believers used to meet together in Solomon's Porch (part of the Temple). There were probably several reasons for meeting in the Temple in the early days; firstly there were so many of them that there could not be many places that were big enough for such a gathering, secondly it was a familiar place to all Jews and thirdly it was a great place to evangelise as so many visited the Temple all the time. These meetings at the Temple only lasted a short time because in around 35AD there was persecution against Christians, Stephen was killed, and there was a scattering of the believers away from Jerusalem.

Acts 2:46 also says that the believers broke bread in their homes and ate together. This custom of meeting in homes continued for some 200 years and is evidenced in several places in the Bible. In 1 Corinthians 16:19:

'Aquila and Priscilla greet you warmly in the Lord, and so does the church that meets at their house.'

In Colossians 4:15:

'Give my greetings to the brothers at Laodicea, and to Nympha and the church in her house.'

In Philemon 2:

'to Apphia our sister, to Archippus our fellow-soldier and to the church that meets in your home:'

And in Acts 20:20:

'You know that I have not hesitated to preach anything that would be helpful to you but have taught you publicly and from house to house.'

.

When the gathering became too big for the house they would plant into another house. The Bible speaks of the church at Antioch (Acts 13:1), the church of God in Corinth (2 Corinthians 1:1), and the church at Jerusalem (Acts 8:1). These churches would have been made up of many gatherings meeting in homes; collectively they were considered one body. Denominations were still five hundred years away.

The meeting in houses was no accident; there was no real reason why they could not have raised up church buildings, in fact it would have been the natural thing to do because as Jews they had met in the Temple all their lives or if they had been pagans they would have met in their Temples. Although there were times of persecution up to the 4th century, there were long periods of peace in all parts of the Roman Empire and yet no church buildings were erected until many years later.

As for the format of the service, 1 Corinthians 14:26 shows that everyone was in the habit of contributing to the service with a psalm, a teaching etc and Colossians 3:16 talks about teaching and admonishing one another and Ephesians 5:19 about speaking to one another with psalms, hymns and spiritual songs. Clearly in these early church meetings each person was expected to and did contribute to the proceedings. Everyone used the giftings that the Holy Spirit had given them to help strengthen one another.

Paul gives a list of some spiritual gifts in 1 Corinthians 12:8-10 and 12:28 and it is clear that Paul considered these gifts as a common occurrence. Each meeting would have had these gifts flowing and the prophetic gifts were widely in evidence. In 1 Corinthians 14:1 Paul says. 'Eagerly desire spiritual gifts especially the gift of prophecy' and in 1 Corinthians 14:29-31:

'Two or three prophets should speak, and the others should weigh carefully what is said. And if a revelation comes to someone who is sitting down, the first speaker should stop. For you can all prophesy in turn so that everyone may be instructed and encouraged.'

One would therefore expect to see the prophetic used extensively during a New Testament meeting. The early Christian would have expected to hear God day by day and use the prophetic to bless and encourage those around him.

In I Corinthians 12:14-27 Paul gives the well known analogy of the body of Christ that is made up of many different parts, hands, feet etc. Each part is vital for the health of the whole body; we cannot do without any one part of the body. Paul ends the analogy in verse 27 when he says, *'Now you are the body of Christ, and each one of you is a part of it.'* This is how the service was; each person is unique and brings his/her special giftings to the meeting. The Holy Spirit flowed through each person and by giving a psalm or teaching etc each person was contributing to the whole. So as each contributed their portion, the whole was an expression of the body of Christ.

I have never experienced this in a church service, but I can imagine that when it is working the way it should the whole is much more than the individual parts. When it all comes together Jesus is glorified and His purposes fulfilled at that particular meeting. It would be so wonderful to experience this each time we go to church with the presence of God being ushered in through each person playing their part.

The meetings of the early Church also helped people grow and fulfil their calling (Ephesians 4:13). Frank Viola says in 'Rethinking the Wineskin.'

'Mutual ministry is the Divine antidote for preventing apostasy; the Divine requirement for ensuring perseverance; and the Divine means for cultivating individual spiritual life.'

Hebrews 3:12-14 says:

'See to it, brothers, that none of you has a sinful, unbelieving heart that turns away from the living God. But encourage one another daily, as long as it is called Today, so that none of you may be hardened by sin's deceitfulness. We have come to share in Christ if we hold firmly till the end the confidence we had at first.'

We are told here to encourage one another daily to avoid sin's deceitfulness.

Encouragement is a form of love, and clearly in the early Church love was pouring out from one to another. The believers were teaching, encouraging and singing to one another; they were eating together, providing for one another and loving one another. What an amazing discipling environment, something the Church has never been able to do successfully. It would be hard to backslide in such a loving, family atmosphere. What a great place to work out the calling on ones life, to be equipped and to go out and fulfil it.

Leadership

What did leadership look like in a New Testament Church? In this section I am trying to discover if anyone had overall responsibility for the Church at this time. In today's parlance I am looking for evidence of an Archbishop over the Church. I am not talking about the diversity of functions that undoubtedly would have existed in the early Church. There is no evidence in the New Testament of there being one leader of any of the churches. The closest there comes to being any leader is in the Jerusalem church. Peter seems to take centre stage to begin with, as the first five chapters of Acts mainly report his movements and his speeches; however, there is nothing that says that he was in command of the church. By Acts chapter seven persecutions have begun, Stephen is martyred and many leave Jerusalem. Acts 8:14 says that the apostles in Jerusalem sent Peter and John to Samaria, so there still does not appear to be anyone in the leadership role at that time. In Acts 9:27 Saul comes to Jerusalem after his conversion and meets with the apostles, but no leader is mentioned. Peter then appears to spend much time ministering away from Jerusalem and when he returns, Acts 11:2 tells us that he was criticised by circumcised believers. Some would say that Peter was the leader of the church in Jerusalem, but I cannot see any evidence for this.

There is a tradition that James, Jesus' brother was the leader of the Jerusalem church. His name first appears in Acts 12:17 when Peter tells the people who had been praying at Mary's house to tell James and the brothers about his escape from prison. The next mention of James is in Acts 15:13 where he speaks on the 'circumcision' issue. What happens here is that the whole church of Jerusalem is gathered together to hear from Paul and Barnabas about their ministry among the Gentiles and whether the Gentiles should be circumcised is called into question by some of the believers. The apostles and elders meet to discuss the situation and after much deliberation Peter addresses the whole assembly, and Paul and Barnabas tell of the miracles there have been in their ministry amongst the Gentiles. Then James gets up and gives his 'judgement'. Although that may indicate that he had the final say, there is every indication in this passage that the whole church was in agreement that Gentiles need not be circumcised. First of all the apostles and elders discussed it for a long time, and they would not have come out to talk to the assembly had they not been in agreement. The whole assembly then became silent as they heard testimonies, a clear sign of agreement and then the apostles, elders and the whole church appointed people to go to Antioch with the decision; another sign of unanimous agreement.

Galatians 2 gives Paul's version of his visit to Jerusalem and he says in verse 2 that he went to speak to those 'who seemed to be leaders.' This is more evidence that even in Jerusalem there did not appear to be any clear leadership structure. James' final mention is in Acts 21:18 when Paul reports to him and all the elders were there. Interestingly there is no mention of the apostles; presumably they were all ministering in different parts by this time. Clearly James does play an important role in the Jerusalem church, but historians are not clear as to why or exactly what his role was. It is likely in the early days of the church that the apostles and close relatives of Jesus would have had a prominent position, but this was an exceptional situation and was not reflected in churches in other parts of the world. This meeting with James took place around 58; James was martyred c 62, the great Jewish revolt occurred in 66 and in 70 Jerusalem was sacked. By 70 Christians in Jerusalem seem to fade away from history and the church there ceased to be of any historical importance.

The description of the meeting in Jerusalem is a good example of how church worked in those days. Everyone from the house churches in Jerusalem assembled together to hear the news from Paul and Barnabas. One of the most crucial decisions in Church history, one that allowed the Gentile church to grow, was made through consensus. Had the decision been to enforce circumcision there would at least have been a split in the Church or many fewer Gentiles would have become Christians. The issue was discussed in depth by, as it were, a board of mature, experienced Christians, with perhaps James as the president, and once they had reached a consensus, the issue and their opinion, was put to the whole assembly. The assembly concurred and the decision communicated to Antioch.

Decisions in the early Church were made by consensus with the Holy Spirit presiding. There do not seem to be any leaders imposing their views on a congregation; the whole assembly made the decision and it worked because the Holy Spirit was in control. I remember reading several years ago of a pastor in the USA who came to his new church and insisted that decisions made by the PCC (Parochial Church Council) would be by consensus. Members of the PCC had never experienced anything like this before and to begin with it was difficult, but the pastor would not allow any decision to be made without 100% agreement. In time they learned to open themselves up to the Holy Spirit and all decisions were made by consensus.

I am trying here to show my understanding of how church was in New Testament times; I am not trying to advocate that all churches today should be run by consensus. If the Holy Spirit was as powerfully present in all churches today as He was then, it might be possible to do that; but today most of our minds are conditioned by the world rather than the Holy Spirit.

Being in unity is a foundational part of the teaching of Jesus (John 17:23) and true unity cannot come from one person imposing his view on others. Matthew 18:19 says:

'Again, I tell you that if two of you on earth agree about anything you ask for, it will be done for you by my Father in heaven.'

The power in agreement is huge and dissenting voices can destroy everything. When everyone is agreed they all take on the responsibility for the decision made, and this stops people from complaining and causing disruption in the congregation. Obviously there are going to be some people who are less enthusiastic than others but everyone will own the decision. It does take longer to make decisions when you are seeking a consensus, but if the Holy Spirit is being listened to, the consensus will come. I assume that this is part of the reason for the commitment to house churches, as it must be much easier for 30 or 40 to reach consensus than 300 or 400. Decision making by consensus is not unknown in the church today with Quakers and New Testament/House churches often using this method.

Church planting and local church leadership

Let us now look at the question of how these churches came into existence. Paul's missionary journeys give a good insight into the process. Acts 14 shows Paul, who had already spent a long time in Antioch, moved on with Barnabas to Iconium, Lystra and Derbe. He spent time in each city winning people to the Lord and setting up churches. Then in Acts 14:22-23 it says:

'strengthening the disciples and encouraging them to remain true to the faith. "We must go through many hardships to enter the kingdom of God," they said. Paul and Barnabas appointed elders for them in each church and, with prayer and fasting, committed them to the Lord, in whom they had put their trust.'

So Paul would evangelise a city and stay there for a while to win more to the Lord and to teach the new believers. He would then leave them for a while to let the new believers mature on their own and then return later to appoint elders in each church. Notice that the word is elders and not elder; nowhere in the Bible does it say that an elder was appointed. All the churches had elders overseeing them and they were called elders, not because it was the title of an office but it described them as being older, more mature believers. Paul would wait and see who rose up in the church naturally, with the qualifications of an overseer (the same as elder) and then appoint them; there was no question of Paul imposing his choice on the people, he would wait until the Holy Spirit made it clear as to His choice and as an apostle he would confirm it.

Titus 1:6-9 and 1 Timothy 3:2-7 describe the character of an elder. Basically he must be blameless and above reproach. This is something we need to pay attention to in these days when we hear reports of pastors involved in immorality etc. Our leaders today sometimes are infected with worldly values. We must remember that although we are in the world, we must not be of it. We need a revival of holiness in the Church of the 21st century.

The fact that there is no vicar or pastor leading a New Testament church is confirmed by the fact that Paul does not write any of his Epistles to a leader. Romans is 'to all the Romans'; the two letters to the Corinthians are 'to the Church of God in Corinth; Galatians is 'to the churches in Galatia'; Ephesians is 'to the saints in Ephesus' etc. Paul does write three letters to individuals but these are mentoring letters and are not to any church. These letters were read out to the whole assembly of the church in the city and some of them, like Galatians, would have been taken from city to city and from town to town.

One of the main jobs of an elder is described by Paul in Acts 20:28-30:

'Keep watch over yourselves and all the flock of which the Holy Spirit has made you overseers. Be shepherds of the church of God, which he bought with his own blood. I know that after I leave, savage wolves will come in among you and will not spare the flock. Even from your own number men will arise and distort the truth in order to draw away disciples after them.'

Paul describes their jobs as shepherds, in that they are to keep watch over the believers, to spot any men who will try to lead them away from the truth.

Another job for the elder is to serve. Many leaders today are in a position where they tend to rule over the congregation, but that was never the Lord's intention;

they are meant to serve. I shall be discussing later how this corruption of God's plan has come about. The principle of serving and not lording over is found all over the gospels; the word 'servant' is used 73 times. Consider Matthew 20:26-28:

'Not so with you. Instead, whoever wants to become great among you must be your servant, and whoever wants to be first must be your slave - just as the Son of Man did not come to be served, but to serve, and to give his life as a ransom for many.'

and Mark 9:35:

'Sitting down, Jesus called the Twelve and said, "If anyone wants to be first, he must be the very last, and the servant of all."'

Jesus came to earth as a servant and we are servants to each other and to unbelievers, and our leaders are servants to us. This really is a principle that has been lost for hundreds of years but, praise God, it does seem that some leaders are now getting the message.

Peter gives very clear instructions to elders in 1 Peter 5:1-3:

'To the elders among you, I appeal as a fellow-elder, a witness of Christ's sufferings and one who also will share in the glory to be revealed: Be shepherds of God's flock that is under your care, serving as overseers - not because you must, but because you are willing, as God wants you to be; not greedy for money, but eager to serve; not lording it over those entrusted to you, but being examples to the flock.'

Elders are to watch over the saints, to serve them and to be examples to them. They are to lead by example; if their characters are blameless then through their mentoring, they will produce fruit like themselves.

I must re-emphasise that there is no office of elder in the New Testament; 'elder' describes his character and his acting as an overseer describes his function. Apart from protecting the saints they would also keep a watch over the services to ensure that there were no excesses exhibited, provide discipline if it were required, communicate with other churches and as a board they would discuss issues of church direction and then put it to the whole assembly.

Another point to make about these elders is that they were not paid; they supported themselves. I assume that they would receive some gifts from time to time, but they were not full time professionals as most leaders are today. Paul made this clear to the elders of Ephesus in Acts 20:33-35 that 'it is more blessed to give than to receive'.

Another role in the church was that of 'deacon'. Deacons were appointed in Acts 6 to serve food to the widows. It was another serving function and the required qualities of a deacon are listed in 1 Timothy 3:8-12. Clearly, like the elders, the character of deacons was of paramount importance.

The teaching in the churches would have been carried out by those mentioned in Ephesians 4:11-12:

'It was he who gave some to be apostles, some to be prophets, some to be evangelists, and some to be pastors and teachers, to prepare God's people for works of service, so that the body of Christ may be built up.'

These may have been anyone in the church or they may more probably have been itinerants like Paul, going from house to house, city to city, preparing God's people. This is known as the 'five-fold ministry' but it may well be a 'four-fold' ministry as many believe that 'pastors and teachers' are one gifting. John Stott in 'The Message of Ephesians' says

'Since the definite article is not repeated in the expression 'some pastors and teachers', it may be that these are two names for the same ministry.' (page 163)

These ministers (servants) would train each believer to have everything they would need to fulfil God's calling on their lives.

Summary

By the end of New Testament times in around 100, the Church largely met in homes. We know that sometimes they met in the Temple as this was a place where Jews would gather, and it is possible, although there is no biblical evidence, that some meetings were held in other public buildings. The Church was self-governing with elders who encouraged, loved and watched over the people of God. There was no leadership hierarchy of any sort; there was only one person at the head of the Church and that was Christ. It functioned as the 'priesthood of all believers' with every person taking their part in the services and the every day life of the Church. It was a family, with all the aspects of a family; loving, nurturing, encouraging, helping those in need, teaching, protecting, sacrificing and disciplining. Perhaps many will not recognise these as attributes of their family, but they are attributes of God's family. Would it not be wonderful to be part of a church like that?

CHAPTER 3

The King James Conspiracy

Some of you by now may be wondering 'how can you say there is no leadership hierarchy in the Bible. What about the bishops mentioned in Philippians 1:1 (KJV) and what about Hebrews 13:7?'

I am going to now show some of the mistranslations in the Bible; mainly in the King James Version. Many of the misunderstandings concerning biblical leadership come from the mistranslation of a few words in the Bible, and I do not believe that this was accidental. Logically this chapter should come in historical sequence later in the book, but it is important to have an understanding of the mistranslations before we look at this subject further.

History of the KJV

King James I came to the throne in 1603 at a time when the most popular Bible was the Geneva Bible, which was in print in English from 1560 to 1644. This Bible was read widely in England, being particularly popular amongst the Puritans and was even read by James I; part of its popularity was due to the footnotes that talked about 'the priesthood of all believers.' This was something that James really did not like as he was a firm advocate of the 'divine right of kings.'

Bishop Richard Bancroft curried favour with the King by opposing Puritanism that generally believed in the 'priesthood of all believers' and in 1604 he became Archbishop of Canterbury. Alister McGrath in his book 'In the Beginning' says 'Bancroft's strategy for coping with James was simple. He would persuade James that the monarchy was dependent upon the episcopacy. Without bishops there was no future for the monarchy in England.' During his reign he said several times, 'No Bishops, no King', believing that the hierarchy in the Anglican Church was crucial to his role as King.

A new Bible authorised by the King would reduce the readership of the Geneva Bible. Bancroft managed to get himself put in charge of the project and he was also responsible for appointing the teams that did the translating. Bancroft set out 15 rules that had to be adhered to by the translators; one of these being that the old ecclesiastical words be kept. The main reason for this rule was that Tyndale, in the first English version of the Bible, had translated the word 'ekklesia' as 'congregation' and not 'church.' Bancroft appointed 54 translators (only 47 finished the project), dividing them into six groups, each one dealing with a section of the Bible. In order to appear fair Bancroft appointed some Puritans but made sure that they were spread among the groups so that they could not have a majority in any group in order to prevent them influencing the end product. Bancroft was clearly determined to load the dice as much as possible so that the end result would further his and the king's aims.

As a final act to ensure a Bible that was suitable for purpose, Bancroft took the agreed final version and made 14 changes. In his control of the project Bancroft did everything he could to make the Bible support his view of a church hierarchy of Bishops etc and their control over the people.

I now set out below the main errors that helped James and the Anglican Church keep control of the people.

Bishop

The word bishop(s) is mentioned five times in the KJV (Philippians 1:1, 1 Timothy 3:1, 1 Timothy 3:2, Titus 1:7 and 1 Peter 2:25), the Greek word being *Episkopos* or *Episkope*. This Greek word literally means *Epi* 'over', *Skopeo* 'to look or watch' and *Episkopos* is translated 'overseer' in Acts 20:28. The other four times *Episkopos* appears in the New Testament it is translated 'Bishop.' Bishop is a fabrication of the translators and it was allowed into the KJV because of one of Bancroft's 15 rules that said old ecclesiastical words had to be kept and 'Bishop' had been part of the Catholic Bible that had been used for hundreds of years.

Episkope is used four times in the KJV (Luke 19:44, Acts 1:20, 1 Timothy 3:1 and 1 Peter 2:12), in Luke and Peter it is translated, 'visitation' (by God); Acts 1:20 uses the word 'bishoprick' but is a mistranslation and should have also read 'visitation'. 1 Timothy 3:1, as mentioned above, should have been translated 'overseer'.

The NIV does not use the word 'bishop' in any of these verses.

Office

This is another word that gives the idea of hierarchy, of them and us; but there is no such word in the Greek. The English word 'Office' appears seven times in the KJV (Luke 1:8, Romans 11:13, Romans 12:4, 1 Timothy 3:1, 10, 13 and Hebrews 7:5.) The Greek and Hebrew words refer to the Levitical Priesthood and Christ's Priestly Office respectively. Of the remainder:

Romans 11:13 *'For I speak to you Gentiles, inasmuch as I am the apostle of the Gentiles, I magnify mine office:'* In Greek the word is diakonia and according to Strong's means 'service'. This word is found 34 times in the New Testament and it means service or ministering on every occasion except Romans 11:13; clearly this has been mis-translated.

Romans 12:4 *'For as we have many members in one body, and all members have not the same office:'* In Greek the word is *praxis* and according to Strong's means 'act'. This word is found six times in the New Testament and is translated 'deeds' or 'works' on all occasions except here.

1 Timothy 3:1 *'This is a true saying: "If a man desire the office of a bishop, he desireth a good work."'* In Greek the word 'office' does not exist. The translators have added the word 'office' to suit the King's purposes.

1 Timothy 3:10 *'And let these also first be proved; then let them use the office of a deacon, being found blameless,'* and 1 Timothy 3:13 *'For they that have used*

the office of a deacon well purchase to themselves a good degree, and great boldness in the faith which is in Christ Jesus.' Again the translators added the word 'office' that never existed in the Greek.

There is no mention of 'office' in any of the above verses in the NIV.

Deacon(s)

Deacon is the translation of the word *diakoneo* and according to Strong's means 'to wait upon'. It appears 37 times in the New Testament and in every case is translated ministering, serving or administering except in 1 Timothy 3:10 and 13 where it is shown as deacon. The translators have managed to turn the one word *diakoneo* into 'have used the office of a deacon'.

'Deacons' appears three times in the New Testament (Philippians 1:1, 1 Timothy 3:8 and 12.) It is the translation of *diakonos* that is translated as servant or minister the other 27 times it appears in the New Testament. I think that we can agree that the office of Deacon, like Bishop, does not exist in the original Greek; it is an attempt by James/Bancroft to try to show a hierarchy in the Church. *Diakoneo* describes someone who serves the congregation.

Overseer(s)

The word Overseer does not occur in the KJV and Overseers only appears once; in Acts 20:28 as mentioned above.

Elder(s)

The Greek word *presbuteros* is translated 'elder' seven times (Luke 15:25, 1 Timothy 5:1-2, 1 Timothy 5:19, 1 Peter 5:1, 2 John 1 and 3 John 1) in the New Testament. The same word translated 'elders' appears 60 times in the New Testament. In the NIV 1 Timothy 5:19, 2 John 1 and 3 John 1 appear as 'elder' because the verses either refer to how one should treat an elder or the letter is addressed to a specific person.

Vine's Expository Dictionary defines *presbuteros* as an adjective. The comparative degree of presbus, 'an old man, an elder' is used of age, whether of the 'elder' of two persons, or more. *Presbuteros* is an adjective, not a noun, and therefore it can never be translated as an office or position. The translators did change the word from 'priest' as it was shown in Bibles before the Reformation to 'elder', as Tyndale had translated it, but they managed to give the word a priestly connotation.

Throughout the New Testament we are asked to imitate Christ, to be holy, to be loving, self-sacrificing etc. Elders of the New Testament were not leaders of the church as we would understand them, they were the older members of the 'body' who displayed the characteristics of Christ, who in love watched over the people, taught them and guided them. They led by example and they led relationally. There was no position of elder in the church. There were just those who people listened to and deferred to because of their wisdom and Christ-likeness.

Rule over

These are some of the most contentious words in the KJV and they appear five times. To rule over someone is against the whole concept of the New Testament where we are told constantly to love one another, to be humble, to defer to one another, etc. Did Jesus act as a ruler over the people? Would He want anyone in the Body of Christ to rule over anyone – no!

1 Timothy 5:17 *'Let the elders that rule well be counted worthy of double honour, especially they who labour in the word and doctrine.'* The Greek word here is *proistemi* and Vine's defines it as 'to stand before, to lead, attend to (indicating care and diligence)'. There is no authority meant by *proistemi*. It appears eight times in the New Testament, including 1 Thessalonians 5:12. Twice it is translated 'maintain', once to do with children and twice with one's house, none of which should be translated 'rule'.

47

Hebrews 13:7 *'Remember them which have the rule over you, who have spoken unto you the word of God: whose faith follow, considering the end of their conversation.'* The Greek word here and in the other two Hebrew verses is *hegeomai* that is defined as 'to lead or to go before as a guide'. This word appears 28 times in the New Testament and is translated as think, count, esteem and chief (in a political situation). Only in these three verses is it translated as 'rule.'

This verse shows the ruling as a present activity and yet in the Greek it is a past activity; it refers to those saints who are dead. The verse continues in the past tense so this is clearly a mistranslation. The saints referred to here are the 'cloud of witnesses' in Chapter 12. Also the word 'over' has been added by the translators. It does not exist in the Greek.

Hebrews 13:17. As above it means 'to lead or to go before as a guide.'

Hebrews 13:24 *'Salute all them that have the rule over you, and all the saints. They of Italy salute you.'* It is worth noting that Paul (I am aware that we do not know if Paul wrote Hebrews) always wrote to the members of the church and not to any leader. Today if there was a problem in a church one would write to the pastor. In New Testament times one wrote to the congregation. This salutation is to those who led by example and who guided the congregation.

In the NIV none of these verses have 'rule over' in them.

Obey

Obey appears 26 times in the New Testament and every time it refers to God, the Word, parents and masters except in Hebrews 13:17. *'Obey them that have the rule over you, and submit yourselves: for they watch for your souls, as they that must give account, that they may do it with joy, and not with grief: for that is unprofitable for you.'*

I think this is the most mistranslated verse in the Bible with the deliberate aim to show the people that they have to obey the King, the Bishops and the pastors. We have already seen that the translation of 'rule over you' is wrong and I deal with 'submit below'. Here the word obey is *peitho*. Vine's says that the 'obedience' suggested is not by submission to authority, but resulting from persuasion. A better translation would be 'allow yourself to be persuaded'.

Submit

Hebrews 13:17 is the only place in the New Testament where *hipeiko* appears. The word means 'to yield voluntarily to those who care for you or to defer'. Therefore the whole sense of this verse has now changed from an authoritarian, controlling demand to a piece of loving advice.

The word submit appears six other times in the New Testament (1 Corinthians 16:16, Ephesians 5:22, Colossians 3:18, James 4:7, 1 Peter 2:13 and 1 Peter 5:5.) The Greek word here is *hupotasso*. According to Vine's there are two interpretations of this word. One is a military term and the other a voluntary giving in or co-operating. I suggest that the military usage that is applied to most of these verses is inappropriate and out of step with everything Jesus has taught us.

Pastor

99% of churches today are led by a pastor, vicar or priest (the rest are five fold ministry churches) but no such office exists in the Bible. You have seen above that neither Bishop nor Deacon exist and elders/overseers are not in the office of leader. The English word 'pastor' only appears once in the KJV, in its plural form in Ephesians 4:11. The Greek word is *poimen* and in this verse it relates to the function in the Body of pastoring the congregation; it is **not** an office or position. *Poimen* occurs 18 times in the New Testament, nine times in the Gospels it relates to a shepherd with his sheep; six times in John 10 it is Jesus the good shepherd and twice it is referring to Christ.

So the KJV perpetuated the errors that had been in the Bible for centuries, errors of interpretation and translation made to try to perpetuate the idea of a hierarchical Church that must be obeyed by princes and peasants alike.

If you would like to read more on this subject then I recommend three sources: 'Who is your Covering?;' by Frank Viola, 'Mega Shift;' by James Rutz and this link http://insearchofacity.org/files/ec.html.

Chapter 4

The Apostles to Constantine (100-312)

Having researched the Bible to find out what the New Testament Church was like I decided to try to trace how, when and why the Church changed to become the Church that many of us experience today. We need to understand the past so that we can help create the new wineskin that God wants us to move into. There are many church models in existence today, but I am mainly coming from an Anglican perspective with its hierarchical structure.

I can best explain what I am talking about by using the illustration of a pyramid shape. The New Testament Church can be represented by an inverted pyramid; the Church is united with a president at the pointed end, then the council of elders, then probably some deacons/servants and then the congregation. The president of the Council is shown at the bottom because he is a servant leader who is encouraging and watching over the people from behind.

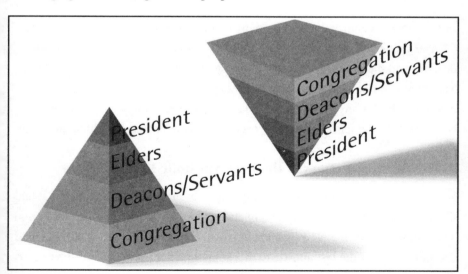

The Church of today looks more like a pyramid standing on its base with the top part (the pastor) separated from the rest of the pyramid and inverted. This shows the pastor out there on his/her own, controlling the congregation. There may or may not be another level of leaders who are similarly detached from the main body. I understand that there are many churches out there that do not conform to this model but generally speaking Catholic, Anglican and many other churches are similar to this model. So how did the model change so much?

There are three main issues that I will try to explain:

1) How did the president/bishop (one among many) become the leader of the church?
2) How did the president/bishop become separated from the rest of the body?
3) How did Episcopacy (hierarchical church) come about?

Please bear in mind that this is a hugely complicated subject on which dozens of books have been written. I am going to try to explain this in a very few pages when normally it takes hundreds and so I will be summarising a great deal, trying to focus on these three questions only.

In the late 19th century there were many historians trying to work out how the Church changed from a self-governing body to one of bishop, presbyters and deacons and then to bishop, pastor and deacons, but none of them could agree. There are just not enough reliable documents for the 60 or 70 years after the death of John for anyone to understand how the transition occurred. I set out below several influences that come together to help answer our three questions.

Letters of the Post Apostolic Period

My first task was to look at the writings dated after the apostolic times that had the most credibility to see if anything changed in the Church during that period. The oldest book of the New Testament is Revelation which was written around 95, and John was the last apostle to die, sometime before the end of the century. The most credible writings immediately after this period are grouped together under the title 'The Apostolic Fathers.' This is a misleading title as it is meant to infer that the authors knew at least one of the apostles and that therefore their knowledge was handed down from them, however it is difficult to maintain this view. These documents were written in the first two thirds of the second century or maybe a little before, and they were first brought together under this title in the 17th century.

It should be noted that historians have discovered several forgeries in the writings that purport to be of the second century. Because of the distance of time it is difficult to tell if something is a forgery or not; so there is some disagreement amongst theologians and historians as to what is genuine and what is not. I will be giving an example of this later. Please remember that all the translations call the president of the council 'bishop'; sometimes I have put bishop/pastor to help us remember that one should not think of the present day meaning of 'bishop'.

I will be looking at only four of the works that are included in The Apostolic Fathers as they are the only ones relevant to my subject. I will look at three now and leave the letter of Clement until later.

a) The Didache

The *Didache* or *The Teaching of the Twelve Apostles* shows how difficult this subject is in that nearly all historians agree that this Christian manual is genuine but there is great dispute as to when it was written because there is so little in it that helps to date it. Some have dated it in the third century but a body of opinion dates it as first century, even as early as 60. This teaching (Didache means teaching) gives a picture of a quite primitive Church, which is why an early date is likely.

For our purposes there are only two paragraphs that shed any light on the internal workings of the Church; the first is paragraph 13 which shows the important position of Prophets in the Church of that time.

'But every true prophet who wants to live among you is worthy of his support...
Every first-fruit, therefore, of the products of wine-press and threshing floor, of
oxen and of sheep; you shall take and give to the prophets.'

Paragraph 15 tells the congregations to elect elders and servants (deacons)

'men meek, and not lovers of money, and truthful and proved; for they also
render to you the service of prophets and teachers.'

There is nothing here to help us answer our three questions.

b) The Letters of Ignatius and Polycarp.

Ignatius is reputed to have been the 'Bishop' of Antioch in Syria, but nothing
more is known of him except through his letters. Tradition has it that he was
arrested in Antioch around 107 and transported to Rome to die in the arena, and
on the way he wrote several letters to encourage the saints. This letter is crucial
to the answer of our questions one and three.

On the face of it the Letters of Ignatius show that the role of the president of
the council of elders had changed substantially by this time. 107 is so close to
the death of the last apostle that if true it is more than likely that this change
would have started during apostolic times. This assumption would not be
good for my contention that the role of the pastor in many churches today is
unbiblical. Most of his letters are stuffed full of references about how they
must obey their bishop and how they must do nothing apart from their bishop;
in fact it would be difficult to imagine that he could have put in any more.
All these quotes are from the more recognised 'shorter' version of the seven
letters. In the Letter to the Ephesians he says:

'It is manifest, therefore, that we should look upon the bishop even as we should
look upon the Lord Himself.'

In the Letter to the Trallians he says:

'For since you are subject to the bishop as to Jesus Christ.' and *'In like manner, let all reverence the deacons as an appointment of Jesus Christ and the bishop as Jesus Christ, who is the Son of the Father, and the presbyters as the Sanhedrim of God, and assembly of apostles. Apart from these there is no Church.'*

And in the Letter to the Smyrnaeans:

'See that you all follow the bishop, even as Jesus Christ does the Father... Let no man do anything connected with the Church without the bishop.' And *'It is well to reverence both God and the bishop. He who honours the bishop has been honoured by God; he who does anything without the knowledge of the bishop, does serve the devil.'*

There are also many references to bishop, presbyters and deacons to show that ostensibly church hierarchy was in place in many churches in Asia Minor at a time just after the apostles.

There are 13 letters from Ignatius in existence and of these 13 there are seven that have a longer, a shorter version and there is a Syriac version of three letters; so we immediately have a problem of knowing which one of the four versions is the genuine article. To begin with it has long been accepted that six of the 13 are forgeries and the longer version of the seven letters is also thought to be a forgery but what of the others? There are 23 different letters or variations of letters and at least 16 of them have to be forgeries as only one of the group of seven letters or the group of three can be genuine, but of course they may all be forgeries.

The Letters of Ignatius highlight the problem of what ancient documents you rely on and what you don't. In various books I have read in researching this subject I have found quotations from the Apostolic Fathers literature with no discussion on their genuineness. We tend to accept far too easily what we hear from teachers and what we read in books. It is very important that we check up on the things we hear and read, and as already mentioned I hope you will check what I have written in this book. I remember my pastor telling us that when he was a young man he could not understand why his pastor never taught on the parts of the Bible relating to spiritual gifts. On asking him the pastor said that they were for biblical times only and not for today. I hope that those of you who are parents regularly check out what your children are being taught at school; teachers are brainwashing our children with dreadful lies about morality and sexuality and we need to correct these lies. A similar example is the way nearly everyone accepts the theory of evolution even though there is not a scrap of evidence to prove the truth of it; but because professors and scientists are considered to be so clever, we accept what they say.

The Letters of Ignatius are particularly controversial because they are the only 'evidence' that Episcopal hierarchy was in place during the early part of the second century. On the face of it they must be true because they are quoted by well known writers of the third and fourth centuries, but on further investigation everything is not quite what it seems and I think that they are all forgeries. The arguments relating to these letters tend to vary depending on whether you are a Catholic/high Church Anglican or not.

At this point I must mention another letter from the Apostolic Fathers collection, Polycarp's Letter to the Philippians, because this is the main evidence used to prove the genuineness of the Letters of Ignatius. Polycarp was the president (Bishop) of the church of Smyrna, and a most respected figure in the Ancient Church. Not much is known of his life but he died a martyr around 167 at the age of 86.

I shall now set out the reasons why I believe the Ignatius Letters to all be forgeries and in this I am much indebted to the detailed work of W D Killen who wrote 'The Ignatian Epistles Entirely Spurious', a reply to the Right Rev Dr Lightfoot, Bishop of Durham. Killen was Principal of a Presbyterian Theological College in Ireland so you can see how the battle lines were drawn. This work was written in 1886 and both men had been studying this subject for around twenty years; it was in answer to a massive publication of 1800 pages by the well known historian Bishop Lightfoot.

A few of the main points are:

1. At the time of the Reformation in the 16th century, Calvin and Oxford and Cambridge Universities thought they were forgeries.
2. In 1644, at the time when Charles 1 was fighting for his crown and for his and his father's (James 1) belief in the 'Divine Right of Kings', Archbishop Ussher brought out a new version of the Letters. This was a timely moment to confirm from history the hierarchy of the Church.
3. Polycarp was only 24 at the supposed date of the Letter of Ignatius to Polycarp. Polycarp mentions an Ignatius in his Letter to the Philippians (hence the 'proof') but there is no way that a 24 year old could have written a fatherly letter to the Church at Philippi; nor would Ignatius have written a letter in the style he did to a 24 year old.
4. Ignatius' letters show a time of persecution and there is no evidence in history that there was persecution around 107.
5. Polycarp mentions 'kings' in his letter and the Roman Empire did not have two Emperors until 161 so there is no way that Polycarp's letter could have been written in 107.
6. The Ignatius in Polycarp's letter is from Philippi and not Antioch. For other reasons also he is clearly not the same Ignatius.
7. In his letter to the Romans Ignatius describes the gory death he is hoping for in the arena. He glorifies his future martyrdom and tells his readers that they must not try to save him. He sounds like a wild fanatic and not a respected man of God.
8. The number of references to bishops being reverenced and looked upon as God does not ring true when there are no other examples of this happening from any other literature of the period. The position of the bishop as described in the letters is so far from what is shown in the Bible that it cannot show the true state of the Church at that time. I think the writer has over played his hand.

There are many other reasons to dismiss these letters as forgeries and the full article can be read on the website at http://www.gutenberg.org/dirs/etext05/8igep10.txt.

Killen argues that the forgeries were probably written in the early third century, a time when many forgeries came out of the Church. He believes they came out of Rome, probably from the hand of a nefarious character called Callistus who had been elected president of the council of elders in Rome in 219 and who was trying to get Church hierarchy established with him at the head. This was also the time when the wrong idea about martyrdom entered the Church; Killen says 'there had been an increasing tendency all over the Church to exaggerate the merits of martyrdom. This tendency reached its fullest development in the early part of the third century.

There is in my mind no doubt that these letters are all forgeries. They were skilfully done and if they did indeed come from the top of the Church in Rome it is small wonder that later historians took them to be authentic, especially as by that time episcopacy had become an established fact. Even the Bishop of Durham admits that there is no sign of episcopacy in the Bible. He says

'It is shown, (referring to his Essay on the Christian Ministry), that though the New Testament itself contains as yet no direct and indisputable notices of a localized episcopate in the Gentile Churches ...'

He goes on to say that there is proof through the Letters of Ignatius. At this point I conclude that there appears to have been little change in the organisation of the Church or in the role of the president up to 160 around when Polycarp's letter was written.

Heresy

In 185 the theologian Irenaeus wrote 'Against Heresies' which was aimed at the heresy of Gnosticism that had plagued the Church for some decades. In this work he brings forth the idea of the truth of the New Testament being handed down from the apostles to the elders and then from elder to elder to the present time. This was to show that the truth about Christ was reliably handed down, so that if you were in a church with a Council of Elders, then you could rely on the teaching as being that originally handed down. He indicated that wherever you were you would be near to a church where an apostle would have taught. The idea was to prevent heresies entering into a church, but it had the unintentional effect of raising the status of the leaders of the churches by putting in their hands the judgement of what was truth and what wasn't.

Two hundred years later, Jerome wrote in around 379 a work against the Luciferians and he makes the same point but he is much stronger about the role of the pastor.

'The safety of the Church depends on the dignity of the High Priest. If to him is not given a certain independence and eminence of power, there will be made in the Church as many schisms as there are priests.' (C. Lucif 9, vol II, 182).

In 387 Jerome spells out his opinion on the position of the 'bishop' in his commentary on Titus.

'A priest is then the same as a bishop; and before party-spirit in religious matters arose by the devil's suggestion, and it was said among the peoples: "I am of Paul, I of Apollos, and I of Cephas", the Churches were governed by a common council of presbyters. But after each of them came to think that those whom he had baptized were his own and not Christ's, it was decreed in the whole world that one of the priests should be elected to be placed above the others, and that to him the whole care of the Church should belong, and thus the seeds of division should be destroyed.'

His comment about 'it was decreed in the whole world that ...' was untrue; being used to emphasise his point. You can see that by this date the leader of the Church has become the exalted person he generally is today.

I can see Irenaeus' point that showing that successive elders have taught the same truths through the generations would help to see off heresy but I do not understand Jerome's point of view that having one man lead and control the Church would have the same effect. It has been shown dozens of times in church history that a congregation or indeed the whole Body of Christ can be led astray or abused through the dominance of one leader. Surely if there were a Council of Elders guiding a church there would be far less likelihood of heresy coming in because one man's peculiar views would not be shared by the rest and therefore not adopted.

Holy Spirit

Thomas Lindsay in 'The Church and the Ministry in the Early Centuries' says:

'The time of enthusiasm had passed away for the great majority of Christians. Unimpassioned conviction took the place of the earlier almost unrestrained passion of faith.'

He is referring to the middle of the second century. I suppose this was inevitable as memories of the days of the apostles faded; it is the same today after a period of renewal or revival the unrestrained passion fades.

From 124 there was a period of freedom from persecution in the Roman Empire and there is no question that Christians began to take on more 'worldly' values during that period. I am not sure what happened; whether the Holy Spirit left many of the people or whether the people left the Holy Spirit; either way there were fewer gifts being exhibited, especially prophecy.

I believe that the general lowering of standards and the withdrawal of the Holy Spirit can be proved by the advent of Montanism. It is important to realise that Montanism was not a heresy; it was something that was inside the existing Church until the movement became a separate Church in the 180s. The movement began around 160 and it received a lot of support from Christians who were not happy with the way the Church was going. They were not happy with the lack of self-discipline, with the sidelining of the prophetic and with the worldly attitude of the Church; they in fact wanted to go back to how the Church was in the early years. The movement began in Phrygia (western Turkey) and many Christians in that area stayed with the movement when they separated. The theologian Tertullian originally supported Church hierarchy but in 207 he went over to the Montanists and began to teach on 'the priesthood of all believers'. The Montanists were persecuted a great deal, much of the time by Christians until they were finally persecuted out of existence around 525.

Montanism was a sign that all was not well with the Church; other similar movements (Anabaptists, Puritans etc) rose up throughout history as a sign that the Church was off track. If the gifts of the Spirit were not flowing through the Church it would be natural for the members of the congregation to feel leaderless. When we hear from the Lord we know the direction we are to take; when we do not hear from Him we tend to look around for help from others. It would be the most natural (although wrong) thing to look to a man to guide them, probably a man who was still moving in the gifts of the Spirit. Remember in the Old Testament how the Israelites insisted that they have a king; it seems to be part of our fallen nature that we are happy to be led.

With the receding of the 'gifts' the service would have taken a very different tone; few people would come to the meeting with a psalm, teaching etc and there would be little prophecy. This meant that in all likelihood people would have turned to the elders to supply the teaching, prayer and the prophetic words that they used to bring through the power of the Holy Spirit. This would have resulted in the beginning of the great clergy/laity divide or the 'them and us' syndrome, which has so crippled the Church of today.

Persecution

Persecution of Christians was seldom widespread or government inspired; it was mainly localised and often begun by a mob. As Philip Shaff says in his

'History of the Christian Church AD1-AD311',

'The common people also, with their polytheistic ideas, abhorred the believers in the one God as atheists and enemies of the gods. They readily gave credit to the slanderous rumours of all sorts of abominations, even incest and cannibalism, practised by the Christians at their religious assemblies and love-feasts, and regarded the frequent calamities of that age as punishments justly inflicted by the angry gods for the disregard of their worship.'

Some Christians were executed during the Emperor Trajan's (98-117) reign but he had firm rules on the subject. He wrote to Pliny the Younger,

'You have adopted the right course, my friend, with regard to the Christians; for no universal rule, to be applied to all cases, can be fixed in this matter. They should not be searched for; but when accused and convicted, they should be punished. … But anonymous accusations must not be admitted in any criminal process; it is a bad example, and is contrary to our age.'

Hadrian (117-138) was mild towards Christians and Antonius Pius (138-161) even protected them from the mobs.

There were two great persecutions under Marcus Aurelius (161-180), the first in Asia Minor in 167 in which Polycarp was martyred and the second in 177 in Lyons and Vienne. Times were quiet again under Commodus (180-192) but under Septimius Severus (193-211) there were many local persecutions.

My point here is that at a time when the Spirit was quiet in the churches it would have been more difficult for people to know what to do. In early Church times people would be encouraging and supporting one another, so in times of persecution there would be a corporate way to face what came against them. However in times when the Holy Spirit was not being heard it is understandable that people would turn to a charismatic leader for advice and protection.

Natural development

The turn of the first century saw the churches with a Council of Elders and possibly a President who was just the first among equals. At the beginning of the second century the words for bishop, presbyter and overseer were still interchangeable. I have found it really difficult in my research to not think of the many references to 'bishop' as meaning something like we understand the word to mean today. It must be understood that the word 'bishop' in the first centuries referred initially to an elder and then later to what we know today as a pastor. Later still the word became used to mean someone in a hierarchical position over the pastor, the same meaning we have today.

Even Irenaeus, at the end of the second century did not draw much distinction between the words. However, it would have been natural in some churches for the president to have been raised up more than the other elders, and I am sure that in different areas of the Empire the development of Church organisation would have varied. It is impossible to make definitive statements on this subject because the Empire was vast and full of different cultures, so regular practices would have differed.

It was the theologian Cyprian who really brought about the rise of the bishops; you can see his point of view by his words:

'The bishop is in the church, and the church in the bishop, and if anyone is not with the bishop he is not in the church.'

Apostolic Succession

The idea that was beginning to formulate in some minds, that the bishop was above everyone else in the Church and had complete authority over the Church, needed some connection with the early Church to make it acceptable; the Apostolic Succession was that connection. In Lindsay's words:

'Apostolic Succession, in the dogmatic sense of that ambiguous term, is the

legal fiction required by the legal mind to connect the growing conceptions of the authority of the clergy with the earlier days of Christianity.'

We saw earlier that Irenaeus first brought the idea of a link between the apostles and succeeding elders with a view to give some stability to the Church and to protect the Church from heresy. However, Irenaeus always believed that the Holy Spirit was imparted to each member of the congregation and not just to the leader because he was in line of succession from the apostles. Cyprian took the idea further.

a) Cyprian

The idea of Apostolic Succession first appeared in the Roman Church (see below) but it was given substance by Cyprian of Carthage. Cyprian is an example of how disastrous it can be to promote a new Christian to lead a church (1 Timothy 3:6). Cyprian was in middle age when he came to the Lord in 248 and he was elected bishop/pastor of the Church of Carthage in North Africa in 250 and was martyred in 258. He was a successful lawyer by profession, as were many of the theologians of that period; and as such he brought to the Church much of his pre-Christian experiences, including his experience of Imperial Government.

Clearly Cyprian was an extremely clever man and one of strong character, who made a considerable impact on Christian thought in the eight years he led the Church of Carthage. Cyprian sums up his views in his Epistle 33 where he says:

'God speaks through the bishop as he formerly spoke through His apostles, and the Church is founded on the bishops, and every act of the Church is controlled by these same rulers.'

Here is the Apostolic Succession that changed the face of the Church for centuries to come, with Cyprian introducing the theory that bishops stood in the place of the apostles. He was saying that instead of the gifts of the Holy Spirit being in every believer, they were in fact in the bishop who possessed the gifts and powers of the apostles!

Cyprian brought the form of Imperial Government into the Church; he gave the bishop the same authority as a governor of an imperial province. This was the beginning of a time when the Church took on many aspects of imperial organisation, culminating in 325 when Christianity became the official religion of the Empire. Bishops were in God's place and they were responsible to Him alone. Cyprian still believed that bishops/pastors should be elected by the congregation and that the bishop should consult with the congregation and the elders when making a decision, but if he disagreed with the outcome then he should go on his own. He also believed that all bishops were equal and that none outranked another, but this situation could never be sustained in an environment where bishops were so far above the elders and congregation. It was inevitable that this authority structure would flow up through the bishops and that eventually the hierarchical structure of the Church would be complete with the Pope on top of the pile.

It was at this time that the idea appeared that only the bishop had the right to 'bind and loose' (Matthew 16:19), as the Lord had given the right to Peter and then the other apostles, and then according to Cyprian, to the bishops who were the apostles of their day. Again quoting Lindsay:

'The bishop was, therefore, according to Cyprian, the overseer of the brotherhood, the provost of the people, the pastor of the flock and the governor of the Church, and all these terms expressed the relations in which he, as supreme ruler, stood towards them. But he was more. He was also the representative of Christ and the priest of God.'

No longer do we have the priesthood of all believers. The bishop was the priest and he acted as an intermediary between the people and God.

Around this time the structure of the Church was changing. Instead of

67

thousands of independent churches, some of them started to align themselves into groups and some bishops/pastors began to look after churches in several villages. With this increased workload some of the bishops started to take a wage from the churches they were looking after because it was now a full time job.

Cyprian's ideas were taken up quite quickly by the Church in general. It just shows how persuasive a huge lie can be when it is tinged with a minimal amount of truth, and how someone can take an idea that another (Irenaeus) has developed for a completely different purpose and twist it for their own aims. I am not sure why his theories were not ignored; I suppose it is natural for leaders to jump at the chance of having more power. Also with the Church getting more into the world it is not surprising that it would take on a worldly organisational structure. Perhaps Cyprian's martyrdom was a reason, as martyrdom was looked upon with excessive admiration at that time. However, it is still deeply depressing that the Church took on the notions of a man who could not possibly have understood the spiritual nature (he may have understood intellectually) of the early Church of Christ in the few months that he had been a Christian, a man who brought so much of the world in with him, a man who clearly did not have a 'renewing of his mind'.

Why is it that time and time again we look to intellectuals to guide the Church? Many times such people have taken the Church down the wrong road. You can see it in the bishops of today; most of them are theologians. If we have to have bishops why can they not be spiritual men full of love? After all they are meant to take the place of the apostles and I do not remember any of them having a PhD.

The result of Cyprian's theories laid the foundation for an efficient organisational structure, but it resulted in the door being closed for centuries to Christians being able to fulfil their calling in Christ, and it opened the door for terrible pastoral abuse.

b) Letter of Clement of Rome

Catholics today cite the first letter of Clement to the Corinthians as proof of Apostolic Succession. There are two letters of Clement to the Corinthians. They are both included in the Apostolic Fathers, but I have ignored the second letter because there are too many question marks over its origin and authenticity. There are several other documents that are attributed to Clement, but none of them are thought to be genuine. Clement is one of the most respected names of this period, but there are so many myths about him that it is difficult to know what is true. About all we know for sure is that he was one of the elders of the Roman Church. He is on all the lists of Bishops that were put together, probably in the late second or early third centuries (see more below), but he does not always appear in the same place. He appears to have been, on average, third on the list after Peter. He may have been the president of the council of elders, but he may have just been the elder who communicated with other churches. The letter does not mention who the writer is, as it is from the Church at Rome to the Church of God at Corinth, but tradition attributes it to Clement. The letter was written around 95 and deals with a problem in the Corinthian church where they had dismissed their elders.

The doctrine of Apostolic Succession is not biblical; as already mentioned there was no hierarchical structure in the Church and Jesus makes no mention of anything remotely like it. The Catholics make two main points to support the doctrine. Firstly, 2 Timothy 2:2:

'And the things you have heard me say in the presence of many witnesses entrust to reliable men who will also be qualified to teach others.'

There is no sense here of truth being handed down from ordained bishop to ordained bishop; Timothy is merely being told that he must train reliable men who are mature and gifted as teachers to pass on the truth to others. These men are not raised up in any way; it is part of the priesthood of all believers.

The second passage to support the doctrine is in Chapter 42:3-5 of 1 Clement which needs to be read together with Chapter 44:1-3:

'And thus preaching through countries and cities, they appointed the first-fruits (of the apostles' labours), having first proved them by the Spirit, to be bishops and deacons of those who should afterwards believe. Nor was this any new thing, since indeed many ages before it was written concerning bishops and deacons. For thus says the Scripture in a certain place, "I will appoint their bishops in righteousness and their deacons in faith." – Our apostles also knew, through our Lord Jesus Christ, and there would be strife on account of the office of episcopate. For this reason, therefore, inasmuch as they obtained a perfect foreknowledge of this, they appointed these (ministers) already mentioned, and afterwards gave instructions, that when these should fall asleep, other approved men should succeed them in their ministry.'

There are several problems with this passage. To begin with, the translations of Clement were made at a time when the only Bible available was the KJV, with the result that words such as 'office', 'bishop' and 'deacon' are used instead of 'title', 'overseer' and 'servant'. Next, those who advocate that this passage shows the doctrine of Apostolic Succession believe that 'when *these* should fall asleep' and 'should succeed *them* in their ministry;' mean the apostles rather than the ministers. Lastly, one cannot take Clement as being completely true; otherwise it would probably have been included in the Bible. In Chapter 5 he talks about '*a wonderful sign of the resurrection... a certain bird which is called a phoenix.*' The phoenix is a mythical bird but Clement believes it to be real. In addition I cannot find anything in the Bible about '*appointing their bishops*'. There is nothing to justify Apostolic Succession here.

There is nothing in 1 Clement that shows that the organisation of the Church had changed.

Metropolitan Churches

M A Smith says in his 'From Christ to Constantine', referring to the end of the second century:

'Power to advise was still strictly invested in the man, not the office. Irenaeus or Dionysius of Corinth pronounced on various matters with an authority based on their personal wisdom and holiness of life, not because they held a certain position.'

However this was to change.

Originally the Church of Rome had no more power than any other church in a major city, but over several decades the heads (now called Bishop) of the Church of Rome wanted to prove that they had pre-eminence in the Body of Christ, so they tried to prove that there was an uninterrupted line of succession from Peter by publishing lists of those who held the post from the time of Peter. One flaw in this idea was that there is no proof anywhere that Peter was the founder of the Church in Rome; he did minister there and he died there, but the church was founded before he arrived in the city. Another flaw is that the first names on the list would have been no more than presidents of the council of elders and not bishops/pastors at all. Having said that, there would have been few people who could have proved this, so it is likely that the lists went a long way to showing that Rome was steeped in apostolic history.

It is unlikely that there was a pre-eminent leader of the Church of Rome until 155 and this was probably due to the Church growing so much that the organisation had to change to cope with the large numbers. The Roman Church flexed its muscles around this time as it entered the 'Easter' controversy, insisting that the Church in the east adopt the Roman dating for Easter. It did not gain any success on this occasion, but it shows that they were trying to impose their supremacy from at least this point of time. Victor, in 196, tried again and demanded that the Asiatics follow the Roman dating, appealing to his apostolic authority, and when they refused he threatened them with excommunication. Much of the church came down on him hard for being so imperious, but he had shown the rest of the Church that the Church of Rome held an important place in the Body.

There were various reasons why the Church in Rome did eventually gain pre-eminence. Firstly, there was the fact that it was the only western church which had an apostolic letter in the Bible. Secondly, Peter and Paul were martyred in Rome. She was also the birthplace of the Roman Empire and for years the Church of Rome had been giving advice on different issues that kept her in the limelight. It would also have helped her that there was a desire to trace the history of Christianity back to apostolic times, so that people could feel secure and heresies could be fought off. Add to this some of the myths that she propagated, like the Church was founded by Peter and/or Paul and we have quite a potent argument. The sheer size of the church would also have been a factor; according to Eusebius by around 250 there was a bishop, 46 presbyters, seven deacons, seven sub-deacons, 42 acolytes, 50 readers, exorcists and door-keepers, and 1,500 widows and poor people under its care. Schaff estimates from these figures that the number of members was fifty or sixty thousand.

Early in the third century, as mentioned earlier, the nefarious Callistus (who had been a crook and a slave) was trying to increase his authority. He made a new rule whereby a bishop could never be deposed or compelled to resign by the presbytery, even if he committed a mortal sin. This is a sign of things to come, however at this time the Bishop of Rome was still called to task by other bishops, so there was some way to go before he became the supreme Pope.

For a while people had looked upon the church in certain cities with a kind of special respect. At the Council of Nicaea (325) the Churches of Alexandria (Egypt), Rome (central and lower Italy) and Antioch (Syria) were recognised as having some authority over their locale. These cities were chosen because they were the capitals of the three divisions of the Roman Empire. Amongst these three cities Rome was given the honorary distinction of being the most important. So little by little Rome claimed, and eventually received, recognition as being the pre-eminent church in the Body of Christ.

Summary

In answer to our first question as to how the president (one among many) became the leader of the Church, we have seen that Irenaeus, through his 'Against Heresies' put into print for the first time the idea of a connection with the apostles. By telling presidents that they were the ones who had to judge what was biblical truth and what wasn't, he opened the door to the idea that they were 'above' their congregation. Cyprian built on this through his teaching of what is now known as the Apostolic Succession, claiming such a position and power for the president that he became first among many.

In answer to the second question as to how the president/pastor became separated from the rest of the body, this was an unintended outcome from Cyprian's teaching. It was inevitable that once pastors were told they were such gifted and important people that they would stop consulting with the elders and the congregation and make decisions for themselves. However, even before this the comparative lack of the power of the Holy Spirit in the people and in the meetings led people to look to the bishop, presbyters etc to guide and lead them, particularly in times of persecution.

In answer to the final question as to how Episcopacy (hierarchical Church) came about, there is not enough information from the first half of the second century to show how this happened. However, it probably developed naturally through the functions of the Church becoming permanent offices, and as churches grew there may have been a perceived need for a formal structure, so the hierarchy of bishop/pastor, presbyter and deacon came into being. It is unlikely that every church had the same structure; there would have been variations. The extension of this structure to areas with the arrival of bishops as we know them today came out of the growth in size and influence of the major centres such as Rome. This also came about as a result of Cyprian's teaching as it would have been natural for pastors to embrace the ideas of power and position and extend them from the town to an area around the town.

Lindsay sums up what the Body of Christ looked like in the early years:

'there were thousands of churches, most of them single congregations, which nevertheless were one Church, not because they had agreed in any formal way to become one, not because there was any polity linking them together in one great whole, but because they had the unmistakable feeling that they belonged to one brotherhood.'

It is easy to think that there were just a few thousand believers in each major town but this is not so; there were many thousands. In 112 Pliny, who was governor of Bithynia, wrote a letter to the Emperor concerning the Christians in his area:

'I therefore postponed the investigation and hastened to consult you. For the matter seemed to me to warrant consulting you, especially because of the number involved. For many persons of every age, every rank, and also of both sexes are and will be endangered. For the contagion of this superstition has spread not only to the cities but also to the villages and farms. But it seems possible to check and cure it. It is certainly quite clear that the temples, which had been almost deserted, have begun to be frequented, that the established religious rites, long neglected, are being resumed, and that from everywhere sacrificial animals are coming, for which until now very few purchasers could be found. Hence it is easy to imagine what a multitude of people can be reformed if an opportunity for repentance is afforded.' (Letters 10.96/97)

Before the persecutions the numbers were so great that the pagan temples were almost deserted. About 100 years later Tertullian wrote:

'If we were, we are so numerous in even your own estimate that we outnumber your soldiers! If you killed us all, who would be left for you to rule?'

And *'We are a people of yesterday, and yet we have filled every place belonging to you—cities, islands, castles, towns, assemblies, your very camp, your tribes, companies, palace, senate, forum. We leave you your temples only. You can count your armies. Our number in a single province will be greater.' (Apologia)*

Some historians estimate that there were over 50,000 believers in some of the larger cities (as mentioned above) and up until the middle of the third century nearly all of them met in homes. They would communicate with one another and they would always be hospitable to one another. The churches in the empire were known throughout this period for their generosity to the poor; they took Christ's teaching on this subject very seriously. Towards the end of this period the Church probably still had many of the characteristics of the Church in apostolic times, although there would have been more of a leadership hierarchy in place, but the clergy would still have been largely self-supporting.

As mentioned earlier, the amount of forgeries and the lack of documents for the first half of the second century make life difficult when studying this subject. I suppose I am a bit of a conspiracy theorist in that I cannot help but think that the Popes, Archbishops and Bishops of later centuries, sitting in all their wealth and power, had every reason to make sure that documents from the past supported their elevated princely positions, and it would pay them to remove from circulation any documents that brought into question their position.

The wealth and power of the Popes and Bishops expanded significantly during the fourth century which we are going to look at next.

CHAPTER 5

The Fourth Century

There was a huge change in the position of Christianity under Constantine. Having been isolated and sometimes persecuted for nearly three hundred years, Christianity suddenly became the official religion of the Roman Empire.

Constantine takes power

From 250 to the time of Constantine there were three great persecutions. Up until now persecutions were mainly localised, but now they were more widespread. The main reason for this was that the Roman Empire was in decline both morally and economically, which meant that the people needed to blame someone. Christianity was growing fast, so the people thought that their gods were not blessing them with prosperity because they were angry with the rise of Christianity. Also, some Romans believed that the Christian Church was dangerous because it was almost a state within a state.

The first persecution of this period was under Decius from 250 to 253 and the second was from 257 to 259 under Valerian (this was when Cyprian was martyred). Valerian's son reversed his father's policy and although Christianity was not an official religion, it was accepted that the Church had the right to own property and conduct its own affairs. The Church then experienced 43 years of peace during which time the Church grew and people of influence and education gave their lives to the Lord. The peace ended in February 303 when the emperor Diocletian instituted the Great Persecution against Christians. There are no historical records that show why Diocletian began the persecution, and it is particularly surprising as both his wife and daughter were Christians and for 18 years of his reign he had not shown any antagonism towards them.

The persecution was not severe in the West because the emperor there did not support it, but in the east it raged for ten years. Diocletian resigned as Emperor in 305 but the persecution was carried on with great severity by Galerius. However, in 313 Galerius became ill and everything changed. The historian Eusebius, who lived through these times, writes:

'As he (Galerius) wrestled with this terrible sickness, he was filled with remorse for his cruel treatment of God's servants. So he pulled himself together, and after first making open confession to the God of the universe, he called his court officials and ordered them to lose no time in stopping the persecution of Christians, and by an imperial law and decree to stimulate the building of churches and the performance of the customary rites.'

He died five days later.

In 306 Constantius, the Emperor in the West, died and was succeeded by his son Constantine. In the east, Galerius died in 311, and after some scrambling for power Licinius became Emperor in the East. In 312 Constantine marched into Italy to defeat an opponent who wanted to become Emperor of the West. There tradition has it that the day before the battle outside Rome, he saw a cross in the sky with the words 'in this sign conquer' and the following day he had a great victory. There is some controversy over this event as there is evidence that he received this sign as a dream rather than an open vision, but clearly something happened. In 324 Constantine conquered Licinius and became sole Emperor of the Roman Empire.

Both Constantine and Licinius were favourable towards Christians and in 312 they issued together the Edict of Milan. This Edict was the first step in establishing Christianity as the religion of the empire (a step taken in 391), giving everyone freedom of worship:

'We had therefore given command that Christians and non-Christians alike should be allowed to keep the faith of their own religious beliefs and worship.'

Except for a short period under Julian, who tried unsuccessfully to bring back the pagan gods, the Catholic Church was to grow in power over the next twelve hundred years until the Reformation. As well as religious freedom the Edict declared that all Church property that had been confiscated by the state or by individuals should be returned:

'*We now decree that if it should appear that any person have bought these places (places where earlier on it was their habit to meet) either from our treasury, or from some other source, they must restore them to these same Christians without payment and without any demand for compensation, and there must be no negligence or hesitation.*'

Another example of the favour given to the Church by Constantine is shown in his letter to Anulinus, proconsul of Africa:

'*So in the province entrusted to you, in the Catholic church over which Caecilian presides, I desire those who give their services to these sacred observances – the people commonly known as clergymen – once and for all to be kept entirely free from all public duties..... In thus rendering wholehearted service to the Deity, it is evident that they will be making an immense contribution to the welfare of the community.*'

The Church for over two hundred years had definitely made an impact on the welfare of the community. During times of famine and disease the churches were well known for the works they did among the poor. During the persecution at the start of the fourth century there are records by the authorities of items held in churches. These inventories show that even small churches would have a considerable amount of food and clothing that was waiting to be given to the poor.

Constantine was an enigma; he was right behind the Church and he said things that made one think that he could be a Christian, but at the same time he worshipped Mithras, the Sun god. After his great victory he erected 'Constantine's Arch' in Rome but there were no motifs about the Lord, only about the Sun god. Some people use the fact that he did not get baptised until just before he died as proof that he was never a Christian. However, there was a theology amongst some in those days that you could only have your sins forgiven once, so they waited until just before death to be baptised so that they could go before the Lord in a pure state. A major blot on his name was the suspected murder of his wife and son at a time when he professed to be a Christian. Other indications of his belief in the Sun god are that he continued to call himself 'Pontifex Maximus' which was the title of the head of the pagan priests, and the sun was still shown on his coins.

I suppose we will never know what Constantine believed. Perhaps his position regarding the Church was a political one; perhaps like many in the fourth century he came to the Lord with all his pagan baggage and allowed it to influence him; or perhaps he cynically kept a foot in both camps. A good example of this is Constantine's setting aside a day of rest every week, but he called it after the Sun god - Sunday. Whatever his beliefs, his actions went a long way to destroy the beautiful New Testament Church. Some of the changes were:

Changes made by Constantine

Some of the changes made were:

a) Church buildings

The first known buildings that were built specifically for church services were around 230, although it is possible that somewhere in the Empire a church building existed before that date. Many of them were burned down in the recent persecutions and so Constantine made a point of building large structures in most of the main towns of the Empire.

The early Christians believed that God was in each of them through the in-dwelling of the Holy Spirit; their bodies being the temple. However, Constantine developed the pagan concept of a space being holy. He built churches on top of the sites of martyrs' graves (such as St Peter's in Rome) and in Christian graveyards. This is where we get the idea of a church being somewhere that is sacred, a place where we must not talk loudly and where we must put on a serious, reverential look. It is small wonder that in many church buildings the joyful nature of the early Church has gone.

His first church was St John Lateran, which copied the architectural style of the Roman governmental building, the Basilica, and subsequently was the model used for churches of this period. The Basilica was a rectangular building with two rows of columns separating the space into three parts, the larger one being the central nave, with a small semi-circle added onto the end, called the apse. You had to go up steps to the apse where the magistrate would sit on a throne and from there make his judgements. Instead of the magistrate there was now the pastor/bishop sitting on the throne, raised up and separated from the congregation, with his elders and deacons sitting in a semi-circle around him.

This style of building emphasised in the physical what Cyprian had taught in theory, that the pastor/bishop was high and lifted up above the congregation, a model that most churches today adhere to. The idea of them (the clergy) and us (the laity) was now given form. Constantine built great edifices in this format across the Empire and others copied the Basilica model until it was the universal design for a church of that period. To carry on the pagan theme Constantine started the practice of naming the churches after saints, just like the pagans named their temples after gods. Also the Basilica was designed so that the sun would stream into the building onto the place where the magistrate/bishop was sitting, another sop to the Sun god.

b) Bishop/pastor

So how did the bishop/pastor fare under Constantine? The answer is, extremely well. Apart from many of them enjoying a new church building, Constantine instituted the custom of the clergy getting paid a salary; also in 313 he exempted the clergy from municipal duties and property taxes and in 321 legalised the giving of money to churches under wills. Constantine's purpose was to free up the clergy so that they could spend all their time dealing with God's business. This resulted in a rush of wealthy men wanting to join the clergy, but Constantine soon closed that loophole and wealthy men were not allowed to receive the tax exemptions.

All this helped to raise up the clergy above the laity so that everyone began to think that the clergy were special and the laity would look up to them. Constantine needed unity and peace in the Body of Christ throughout his Empire. To this end he instigated several synods (meetings of Bishops) to sort out exactly what a Christian was to believe, so that heresies would be stamped out and all would be of one mind. This strategy was only partly successful, but to help achieve this Constantine banned house churches:

'The emperor, however, enacted a law that their own houses of prayer should be abolished; and that they should meet in the churches, and not hold church in private houses, or in public places. He deemed it better to hold fellowship in the Catholic Church, and he advised them to assemble in her walls. By means of this law, almost all the heresies, I believe, disappeared.' (Sozomen's ecclesiastical history 440 book 2 chapter 32.)

If everyone had to worship in church buildings so that the Church could better control what was going on, then there must have been a significant merging of House churches as there could not possibly have been enough church buildings to go around. It must have taken some time to implement this law. Also, despite the abolition of the houses of prayer, some must have remained in the countryside as the villages would have been too small to afford a new building. However, the result of this law would have meant an increase in size of churches and therefore an increase in the prestige of the bishop.

c) Paganism in the Church

The problem of paganism began right at the start of the Church. After Pentecost there were three types of believer, Jew and Gentile (Pagan and non-Pagan).

* **Theologians with a Greek mindset**

Early on the Church was predominantly Jewish, but as more and more Gentiles joined, the balance soon changed with former pagans predominating. Until I researched this book I had no idea of the importance of the difference between the Jewish mindset and the Greek mindset. I am glad to have found some study notes on the web on 'The Greek versus the Hebrew Mindset'. (http://www. elshaddaiministries.us/studynotes/t22greek_vs_hebrew_mindset.html).

I mention below that it is likely that the first leaders of the churches were Jews who had received a lifetime of training in the 'Word'. Their mindset would have been very much in line with that of Jesus, who was of course also a Jew. The Hebrew looked at life from a unified perspective, believing that reality was both in the physical and spiritual realms, that neither was inferior to the other. He would look at the creation description in the Bible and believe it for what it says; he would accept the literal meaning of what he was reading. Of course the Jew who became a Christian was able to understand the teachings of Jesus and the Apostles far better than we can today, because they would have been able to understand the Jewish nuances, and they did not have to understand the historic situation in which they lived, because they were living it.

The Greek mindset was very different. All the educated Gentiles would have been brought up studying the philosophers such as Socrates, Plato and Aristotle, who lived in and around the fourth century BC. At this time Plato was probably the most popular, and he taught in his 'Theory of Ideas' that you could define anything, including truth. He believed that reality existed in the realm of ideas and that there are two sides to life - the physical and the spiritual, with the former being far superior to the latter. He taught that what people saw, touched and sensed were not really reality; there was a truth behind that reality that caused believers in this teaching to look for the truth behind everything.

Those who were steeped in the teachings of Plato found it very difficult to believe that Jesus was both human and divine. They thought that the body was a prison, it was unimportant; it was the spirit that was all important. This misunderstanding was the source of heresies like Gnosticism and Docetism and several disagreements within the Church over the definition of the Trinity.

Throughout Church history, with the glittering exception of the apostles, the leaders of the Church have been found in the intellectuals of the day. Unfortunately the intellectuals of the second, third and fourth centuries mostly grew up as pagans, studying the works of Plato etc. Although many of these leaders were passionate Christians, they filtered their Christian thought through the Greek mindset of the philosopher. Many thought that there was truth within Plato's teachings and so they assumed that these truths would be in perfect harmony with the truths of the Bible, so they blended them together.

These Christian intellectuals were far more deadly to the Church than the heresies that were discovered and dealt with. As mentioned already, Cyprian had some ideas that were devastating to the Church that came from his Christian ideas being filtered through his pagan mindset. This was a problem that constantly beset the Church over the coming centuries. Justin the Martyr, Tertullian, Origen, Cyprian and Augustine all studied the teachings of the Greek philosophers. Tertullian spoke out severely against philosophy in the Church, but even he was guilty of letting his background influence his writings; he just could not help it. These men were all theologians; the Concise Oxford Dictionary defines 'theology' as:

'The study of the nature of God and religious belief.'

Theology, by its definition comes out of Platonism; the Jews would never consider the need to study the nature of God. They would just want to do what He commands and serve Him. The theologians of these first centuries looked behind the texts for hidden meanings and brought pagan thinking right into the heart of the Church. Because they were intellectuals they were listened to and

84

the effect on the Church was dreadful. Dr R D Heidler highlights this in his new book 'The Messianic Church Arising' when he says:

'Perhaps the most distressing change made by the church fathers, as they filtered biblical truth through their pagan mindset, was that they redefined the way of salvation. According to the Bible, salvation comes by 'believing in Jesus'; when this was reinterpreted through the intellectual Greek mindset, the wording changed from 'believing in' to 'believing that.' According to many of these writers, salvation comes by 'believing that' certain doctrines are true.' (pages 53,54).

It was easier for them to believe that they could attain salvation by believing some dogma rather than submit to the Lordship of Jesus. I suppose I have a rather simplistic view of things. I like to think that God gave us a Bible that we can all understand at whatever level we are at, without the need to try and see what God might have meant about something that He might not want understood until the time He decides to give revelation. In recent years the Lord has been revealing more of His plans and purposes. Spirit-filled theologians are very helpful to pastors and leaders when they feel that they have new revelation from the Lord, in that they can help the leader discern whether what they are sensing is a heresy or indeed from the Lord.

Sadly this Greek mindset is still with us today; in fact it is with most people who were born in the West. The early nineteenth century saw a resurrection of the god of logic and the god of reason, and it has remained with us ever since. I cannot tell you how many times I have told people about incredible miracles that I have either read about, seen or been used by the Lord to bring about and they have looked at me with disbelief. Many say that they would believe it if they could see it for themselves. They had to reason it through, find the logic in what I was saying, but had nothing to measure it against.

Here are some of the characteristics of a Hebrew mindset: relationships rather than knowledge are all important; a love of community rather than individualism; believes in faith and trust rather than requiring proof; believes in the supernatural rather than only believing what one sees, hears etc; believes in spiritual warfare; believes in a moral way of living rather than in creeds and doctrines. I believe that it is our Greek mindset which is responsible for the comparative lack of healings by the Holy Spirit in the West compared with Africa, South America etc. We are always questioning and reasoning; how can the Holy Spirit do His work when we are so unbelieving? I heard someone at a meeting say that he constantly says 'Lord, heal me of my unbelief'; that is a pretty good prayer.

- **Christianity made legal**

As already mentioned Constantine seemed to want the best of both worlds. On the one hand he would promote Christianity wherever he could and on the other he promoted the sun god, Mithras. However, from this time there was a huge growth in the Church and an equivalent decline in overt paganism. The tax and other benefits that he gave the clergy resulted in a rush of people becoming Christians, and this was added to in 325 when he encouraged all his subjects to become Christians. The final influx came in 391 when the Emperor Theodosius declared Christianity the official religion of the Roman Empire and closed pagan temples in Rome.

Although this was a time of huge Church growth it was also a time of unparalleled growth in paganism within the Church. The previous three hundred years had been a time of discrimination, and sometimes of persecution; therefore becoming a Christian took a lot of thought and a lot of guts. Nobody would have joined a church for the benefits and prestige they would receive; no, they would have had a conversion experience and would have joined a house church, joyfully accepting Christ as their Saviour. Everything, though, had now changed; people were joining the Church because it was the trendy thing to do and because there would be benefits to their joining, and later because it was illegal to be a pagan.

It was probably a similar situation to what nearly took place a few years ago in India, when the lowest caste, the untouchables, were fed up with being Hindus, as the religion had not benefited them at all. Their leaders therefore looked around for another religion to join; finally narrowing their choice to Christianity or Buddhism. They chose Buddhism, but had they chosen Christianity, on a chosen day, many millions of Indians would suddenly have become Christian! Virtually none of them would have had any understanding of what they were 'signing up' to and giving their lives to Jesus would have been meaningless.

This is what happened in the fourth century; a huge number of people suddenly started to call themselves Christian, but had no understanding of what that meant. Many of them remained pagans in all but name. K S Latourette illustrates the situation in his book 'A History of Christianity':

'Here and there sites sacred to pagan divinities were appropriated by Christians and were still regarded as hallowed, but by Christian saints rather than by the gods. In at least one place the temple of a non-Christian god was transformed into a Christian church and the latter was devoted to that god thinly disguised by prefixing the title 'Saint' before his name.' (page 209)

• **Superstition**

Through this great influx of pagans there arose superstition and mysticism in the Church. There were signs of this before the fourth century, but it greatly increased at this time. As mentioned earlier, the Martyrs were held in high honour, with their graves sometimes being used as places of worship. Latourette describes the situation:

'When in the fourth and fifth centuries, after the last persecutions, converts flooded into the Church, they tended to transfer to the martyrs some of the reverence they had given and powers which they had ascribed to the gods of paganism.'

This was the beginning of relics being valued and ascribed with mystical powers. There is some biblical basis for this (2 Kings 13:21) when a man came back to life after touching Elisha's bones, but most of this would have been mere superstition. These superstitions further developed into pilgrimages, the sale of relics and praying to the Saints.

- **Giving**

Something else that changed at this time was the attitude towards giving. As already mentioned, the Church up until Constantine was renowned by believers and pagans alike for being generous towards the poor. Today, when we talk of giving we generally speak about 'tithing'. Tithing is now used to support the clergy, maintain the building and give to the poor, but at the beginning of this period there is no evidence in literature that tithing existed. Stuart Murray in his book 'Beyond Tithing' has researched the writings before Constantine and has found the first mention of tithing around 250 in Cyprian's Epistle 65.1:

'The form of which ordination and engagement the Levites formerly observed under the law... Which plan and rule is now maintained in respect of the clergy, that they who are promoted by clerical ordination in the Church of the Lord may be called off in no respect from the divine administration, nor be tied down by worldly anxieties and matters; but in the honour of the brethren who contribute, receiving as it were tenths of the fruits, they may not withdraw from the altars and sacrifices, but may serve day and night in heavenly and spiritual things.'

Cyprian is not saying that tithing is a requirement to support church leaders; he is just showing the type of giving that is needed from the congregation if leaders are going to be full time. Murray concludes that there are very few references to tithing in the writings up to Constantine, and the almost complete silence on the subject for 300 years tends to suggest that tithing was not taught at this time. References to Old Testament tithing began to appear at the end of the fourth century; however it was not until the eighth century that tithing was universally accepted. Tithing is only loosely within the scope of this book, but it is worth asking the question, 'Why do we still accept a teaching on a subject that was not practiced (for the sake of balance it is possible that some people did practice tithing, there is just no record of it in the literature of the time) until around five hundred years after Christ and then only because Constantine changed the position of the pastor and the Church?'

To be fair to Constantine, some of his changes were aimed at giving the clergy the opportunity to work full time in looking after their flock. At this time it appears that congregations grew substantially due to house churches closing and a large number of new Christians coming into the Church, creating a lot more work for the clergy. In order to cope with this change, the clergy had to be paid if they were to work full time. In addition the church buildings had to be maintained, so the implementation of tithing over the next centuries as a means to finance this makes some sort of sense. However, most of the tithing would have been unnecessary if the house church system had been maintained.

So if tithing did not exist at this time, how were the clergy and the poor supported? In the period before Constantine there were very few churches and the clergy were generally self-supporting, so most of the money given by believers went to the poor. We have already seen that in the very early Church they had 'everything in common' (Acts 2:44). It is easy for one to suppose that this was a one-off state that existed in the first flushes of enthusiasm following Pentecost, but there is evidence that this sort of giving continued through the second and third centuries. In Clement's letter to the Corinthians, chapter 55, it says:

'We know many among ourselves who have given themselves up to bonds, in order that they might ransom others. Many, too, have surrendered themselves to slavery, that with the price which they received for themselves, they might provide food for others.'

Dionysius of Corinth wrote a letter in 170 to the head of the Church of Rome complimenting the Roman Church for their usual generosity in sending supplies to many churches that resulted in relief for the poor and for those in the mines. We have already seen that in 250 the same church was looking after 1,500 poor people.

Obviously not all believers were giving in a radical way. Nonetheless, there is enough evidence to suggest that there were a number who gave selflessly, otherwise the Church would not have gained the reputation it did for generosity to the poor. However, times were changing. Murray points out that:

'By the third century new attitudes to wealth and new approaches to giving and sharing were gaining ground in the churches. Radical generosity and a deep commitment to sharing resources within and beyond the Christian community were still evident, but the church was still coming to terms with the influx of rich converts who were reticent about adopting such community practices.' (page 128)

The number of wealthy men greatly increased on the legalisation of Christianity and increased again when Christianity became the state religion. Many of these 'believers' were Christians only in name, so it would have been impossible for them to understand and receive the teaching on sacrificial giving. As a result the teaching on giving changed. Murray again:

'Theologians raided the Old Testament and various secular philosophies to develop a new system that would be acceptable in a much broader church.' (page 129)

I suppose it was a logical step to look at the Old Testament for guidance because the Roman Empire had become a Christian state, just as Israel was a Jewish state. So they brought in the concept of 'tithing' that was so successful in Old Testament times. The most destructive change was the focus on the giver rather than the recipient. The spiritual benefits to the giver were emphasised as opposed to the biblical requirement to look after the poor. This is still with us today as we focus on sowing and reaping. This is a direct result of the watering down of the teachings of the New Testament to accommodate those coming into the Church who are not really Christians. Does this sound familiar? Are some churches not doing the same thing today with regard to turning a blind eye to immorality; watering down God's teachings to accommodate them?

I personally do not like the term 'tithing' as it is too limiting and too controlling; we should drop the word and instead concentrate on teaching that everything we have belongs to God and that we should give according to His will. Tithing is an emotive subject, and there are many different opinions on this in the Body of Christ. Each person believes that their view is biblical. I personally think that giving is a heart issue and we need to try to get away from such 'religious' words as 'tithing'.

- **Images and Saint adoration**

Pagans were used to worshipping objects, both large statues in their temples and small figurines in their homes. The new converts were allowed to change things to suit their way of worshipping and soon the churches were filled with images of the Saints.

Pagans were also used to worshipping many gods, and the custom was brought into the church as well in the form of praying to the saints. The most significant instance of this was with regard to the Virgin Mary.

In New Testament times the main pagan god was Diana, and the centre for that worship was in Ephesus. Originally the Ephesians worshipped Artemis, but the Romans conquered them in the first century and renamed the religion Diana after a Roman goddess. The widespread nature of this religion can be seen in Acts 19:27:

'There is danger not only that our trade will lose its good name, but also that the temple of the great goddess Artemis will be discredited, and the goddess herself, who is worshipped throughout the province of Asia and the world, will be robbed of her divine majesty.'

The Temple was considered one of the ancient wonders of the world. It was four times bigger than the Parthenon in Athens, measured 130 yards by 60 yards and had 127 massive ionic columns that stood 60 feet tall. Make no mistake, Diana worship was a proper religion and behind it were dark spiritual forces.

The Bible talks of the successes Paul had in his ministry in Ephesus and the rest of Asia Minor in Acts 19:10-11:

'This went on for two years, so that all the Jews and Greeks who lived in the province of Asia heard the word of the Lord. God did extraordinary miracles through Paul.'

At that time Ephesus was a large city of around 250,000 people and tradition has it that John took Mary there to live. The city was transformed from a pagan city into a largely Christian one. Peter Wagner says in his book 'Confronting the Queen of Heaven' that within 50 years of John being there:

'Hardly anyone in the Roman Empire worshipped Diana any more. Her cult was reduced to a mere shadow of what it had been before Peter and John went to Ephesus. The city of Ephesus became the centre of world Christianity for the next 200 years!' (Page 21)

Diana was also known as the Queen of Heaven and the Moon goddess, and was represented by a statue of a many breasted woman who has a crescent moon necklace. The crescent moon can also be seen today on the flags of most Islamic nations. Probably the only place in the Bible where God commands us to not pray for someone is in Jeremiah 7:16:

'So do not pray for this people nor offer any plea or petition for them; do not plead with me, for I will not listen to you.'

Verse 18 tells us who He is referring to:

'The children gather wood, the fathers light the fire, and the women knead the dough and make cakes of bread for the Queen of Heaven. They pour out drink offerings to other gods to provoke me to anger.'

Later in Jeremiah 44:4, again referring to offerings to the Queen of Heaven, God says:

'Do not do this detestable thing that I hate!'

Do not think that these ancient gods were just statues without power; no, they were demonic principalities, with the Queen of Heaven being one of the biggest. As already mentioned some pagans just swapped the names of their gods and carried on their pagan worship, only calling themselves Christians. This is likely what happened with Diana worship; some of her devotees would have carried on worshipping the Queen of Heaven, just changing her name to a Christian female 'goddess', Mary. When people worship Mary, their prayers are in fact going to the counterfeit entity that replaced Diana worship.

This Mary worship appears to have got so confused within Christianity that the Catholic Church took it over almost entirely. Firstly, there is a statue of Diana, the many breasted woman, in the same room in the Vatican as statues of the Apostles. Secondly, Mary worship was so prevalent that there was a Church Council held at Ephesus in 431 where the Church officially entitled Mary 'the Mother of God' (one of the names of Baal.). Lastly, there are many images of the Virgin Mary either standing on a crescent moon or with one encircling her head.

Clearly pagan worship is still alive today within the Catholic Church. Peter Wagner gives a very worrying statistic:

'Many were shocked when the August 25, 1997 'Newsweek' magazine reported that in the last four years the pope has received 4,340,429 signed petitions encouraging him to declare officially that the Virgin Mary is the 'Co-Redemptrix or co-redeemer with Christ'.' (Page 47)

93

• Pomp

The high church pomp and ceremony came through Constantine bringing in the pomp of the Imperial court, which was originally part of Emperor Worship, into the Church, most of which came from the customs in pagan temples. Processions, processional music, choirs, special clothes, candle sticks and incense all came into the Church at this time.

All these things put a bigger wedge between the clergy and laity, and this was increased by the rituals that were added bit by bit. The clergy were part of all the pomp and ceremony and the laity just stood to the right and left of the church and watched. At least the laity was able to participate in the worship, but that did not last long because the Council of Laodicea (367) stated:

'No others shall sing in the Church, save only the canonical singers, who go up into the Ambo and sing from a book.' (Canon XV)

So the choirs soon took over all the singing in the Church.

• Immorality

There was a distinct lowering of morals through the proximity to paganism. When Christianity became legal Christians were able to get good positions in government. This mixing with the 'world' created a compromising attitude that still exists today. Also, together with the rush of nominal Christians into the Church, came their pagan morality and the inevitable compromise. There is no question that over time the higher Christian moral standards had a positive effect on the morals of the empire, but at the same time those Christian moral standards were lowered. Several of the decrees that came from the various Councils that met over the next hundred years dealt with immorality amongst the clergy.

- **Monasticism**

With the legalisation of Christianity and the influx of nominal Christians, (as already mentioned), the morals, passion and radical nature of the Church was compromised. Just as with Montanism of the mid-second century, a group of people were unhappy with the worldliness of the Church so they decided to set themselves apart. These people were much influenced by the pagan idea that the body was the cause of sin in one's life, so many took on an ascetic lifestyle in order to get closer to God. They denied their bodily needs to concentrate more on the spiritual, an example of the dualistic teaching of Plato. There were two types of ascetics: one based on a fourth century Egyptian called Anthony, who taught that one should live one's life alone; the other began with another fourth century Egyptian called Pachomius, who taught that one should live in community. Monasticism would play an important role in the later Middle Ages with regard to education, hospitals etc.

- **The sermon**

The sermon we know today did not exist in the New Testament. Most of the speeches were evangelistic in nature, such as Peter's speech at Pentecost and Paul's speeches in various synagogues; the remainder were one off occasions, such as Stephen's speech before he was martyred. David Norrington in his book, 'To Preach or not to Preach?' has researched the early literature and says:

'The evidence from the New Testament and sub-apostolic literature which we have so far examined suggests that the sermon appeared only as an occasional item – an extra, delivered to deal with a specific problem needing attention or on a special occasion. There is no clear evidence for regular sermons'. (page 13)

The Jew's main place of worship was in the home. Each Friday evening the father of the household would lead his family in a service in their home. In the first century the Jewish children were taught the importance of learning the Old Testament scriptures and they learned large portions of them by heart. There was a tremendous emphasis on the Word of God; from an early age the children would go to the Synagogue schools to study the Torah. Heidler in his book 'The Messianic Church Arising' makes an interesting point:

'Because of the Jewish tradition of family worship, it was normal for almost any believer to feel comfortable leading in prayer, worship and the discussion of God's word. This provided the early church with a large pool of potential leaders. When 3,000 people were added to the church in Acts 2, most of these men and women came into the church already accustomed to taking spiritual leadership in a 'home group' setting.' (page 61)

This could be a good reason why the house church worked so well and was so popular; however, as far as teaching is concerned, it is likely that people were taught by the 'father' of the house or by those displaying a teaching gift. As the influence of the Holy Spirit began to recede around the middle of the second century, services would have been organised by 'man' and there would have been fewer opportunities for teaching gifts to be recognised. At the same time the transient apostle, prophet, evangelist and teacher faded into history, leaving the teaching ministry to be done in-house.

Into this void came the sermon. The sermon comes directly from Greek and Roman rhetoric. Rhetoric is an art form that began in Greece, and those who were good at it earned considerable fame and fortune. It was more of an entertainment, and in the second century it relied more on style and presentation than on content. Teaching in the early Church would have involved questions and answers, so that the meat of the subject could be properly understood, but rhetoric was more to do with persuading those listening of a point of view rather than teaching truth. Rhetoric tended to be more about how well the speaker performed than what he said.

It appears that sermons became a regular part of the service around the end of the second century. The sermon was used, unintentionally, to bring corrupting pagan ideas into Christian doctrine. Many of the Church fathers of this period were professional rhetoricians before they became Christians, including Tertullian, Cyprian and Augustine. Many brought philosophical ideas into their writings, including Clement of Alexandria, Origen, Ambrose and Augustine. Even Tertullian, who claimed to despise pagan philosophy, was influenced by it.

This pagan mindset meant that these Church fathers tried to find the hidden meaning behind the Bible verses. They believed that there was a literal meaning and an allegorical one. An example of this would be how for years they would discuss the divinity of Christ and the exact meaning of the Trinity; they would try to analyse God, try to define him.

So by the time of Constantine the sermon was in regular use, given mostly by the bishop and delivered from a raised position in the church buildings that had been newly erected. It was the beginning of indoctrination replacing Bible teaching, bringing with it pagan ideas that should have had no part in Christian doctrine. The sermon also re-enforced the 'them and us' situation by adding to the aura around the bishop, that he is the one with all the knowledge and the only one qualified to teach his flock.

By this time virtually everything that was found in a church building and everything in the church services (except the Lord's Supper) were of pagan origin. Looking at most churches today, you will find the same situation.

d)   The loss of the Messianic Church

I recently read the book by Heidler mentioned above and, to be honest, up to that time I had never really considered that the Church had had any Messianic nature to lose, but his book opened my eyes to some things.

Constantine did not like the Jews and issued orders to sever connections with them. In Eusebius' 'Life of Constantine', Book 3, Chapter XV111, there is a letter from Constantine to the churches after the Council of Nicea in 325 that says:

'Let us then have nothing in common with the detestable Jewish crowd.'

This decree did not have altogether the effect that Constantine was looking for, because disobedience to his law was so prevalent that Church Councils for the next 450 years continued to decree that clergy should not celebrate Passover with the Jews or other Jewish festivals or keep the Sabbath. The penalty for breaking these decrees was to be thrown out of the ministry. The lack of success in stopping churches from keeping connections with their Jewish roots shows that these connections must have gone very deep. Eventually all links between the Church and her Jewish roots were cut, but what did the Church lose by this?

Heidler highlights four things that the Church has lost. Firstly, the awe of God was forfeited. We have already seen how the pagan philosopher theologians have tried to dissect God so as to put Him in neat little boxes. The early Church, like the Jews, were only interested in how to serve Him. The second lost ingredient was a love of the Word. Again, we have already seen how the Jewish family learned the Scriptures by heart, and so it would have been in the early house churches. By the end of the fourth century churches would have been led by pastors who believed that the clergy and an odd layman were the only ones qualified to teach the Bible. It was not long before most of the congregation would have lost the will to study it for themselves.

The third ingredient that was lost was the Judaic emphasis on the home. As mentioned, the Jewish family unit was the basis of the New Testament Church, so when all these churches were built under Constantine the love, fellowship, support etc that existed in the house church was lost. Lastly, the Hebraic attitude to life was lost. The original character of the Church was one of joy, but this all disappeared with the grand churches that required solemnity and decorum. Gone were the times of dancing, love feasts and free worship.

There is no doubt that when we split with our Jewish roots we lost a lot; we lost the true nature of the New Testament Church.

Summary

The Catholic Church, as it entered the fourth century, was becoming a hierarchical organisation (completely against the Lord's design Matt 20:25-28). There were often at least three levels of clergy in the church. There was also a growing hierarchy amongst the bishops as churches gained more wealth and prestige and began to have influence over areas wider than where their church was situated. The Council of Nicea (325) gave the bishops of churches in the major cities authority over the bishops in their provinces. The groupings of churches tended to be based on the administrative districts of the Empire. The word 'Catholic' had been in use since the second century in the context of 'universal' and 'orthodox', it was used to differentiate the Church from other sects who did not look at Christianity in the same way. The division between the clergy and laity was almost complete, and this again came from the pagan mindset that wanted to split life into spiritual and secular, something that did not exist in the early Church. So the 'priesthood of all believers' was dead; ministry was now for the elite.

So by the time Constantine legalised Christianity its organisational format looked very similar to that of the Imperial Government. Christianity was a good option for Constantine as it would replace the religious pluralism that existed in the Empire and give it more stability. People believed in many different gods, but Christianity, with its similar organisational structure, would fit better into an Empire that generally had a common language and a common culture.

If Constantine was going to promote and show favour to Christianity, then he needed to control it as best he could. A divided Church was of no use to him, as it would cause trouble in his Empire, so he called several Councils to try to unify the Body by producing creeds that everyone could accept. As the instigator of these Councils he was allowed to attend and give input, even though he technically was not even a Christian because he had not been baptised. The Emperor had a lot of power over the Church, but it was never as subservient to the Emperor as were the old pagan cults. In 390 Ambrose, Bishop of Milan, excluded the Emperor Theodosius from the Church until he had made due penance for the massacre he had recently perpetrated.

The Church, with its similar organisational structure to the Imperial Government, had become an institution by the end of Constantine's reign. Gone were the vibrancy, love and passion of the New Testament Church, and in their place came inflexibility, control and solemnity. In the place of a united family had come division; them and us; in the place of a home had come a basilica. Instead of mutual support there was hierarchy; in the place of the Holy Spirit there was ritual. As we have inherited the Church of the fourth century and not that of the first, it is small wonder that we find it so difficult to get equipped, envisioned and sent out to fulfil our calling.

In this new environment the needs of the people were subordinated to the needs of the institution. No longer were people built up, equipped and sent out; no, their job was to listen and obey the clergy and support the organisation. One on one evangelism virtually died, after all by the end of the century Christianity was the official religion of the empire and paganism was illegal, so there was little competition. By 500 nearly everyone in the Empire considered themselves a Christian. After three hundred years of Christianity being intermittently persecuted, Christianity became the persecutor. Pagans were killed and their temples torn down by Christians who wanted to get rid of the competition by force and not through evangelism.

Nominal Christians (those who joined the Church because it was the 'thing to do') flooding into the Church unquestionably diluted Christianity to a crippling degree, because they had a false view of God and a world view that was generally in opposition to Christianity. The transition was made very easy for the pagans, as they were allowed to incorporate so much of their religion into the Church. The fourth century is supposed to be the time of the great victory of Christianity over paganism, but I wonder who had victory over whom?

Having said all this, God must have known that the Gentile mindset would direct the Church on a different course, so it must be possible for us to still fulfil God's purposes.

CHAPTER 6

Christianity in Britain

We have looked at the Church for the first four centuries in the Roman Empire, and now we are going to look at Christianity in Britain. There is a lot of Christian history attached to our nation, but we will only be looking at a few specific areas that will help us understand why the Church is so different today compared with New Testament times.

Whitby (664)

Tradition has it that Christianity came to England a few years after Christ's crucifixion and developed strongly under Roman occupation. According to Tertullian, around 200 Christianity had spread beyond Hadrian's Wall into Scotland:

'Parts of Britain were inaccessible to the Romans but have yielded to Christ.'

The Church in Britain in the fourth century did not succumb to many of the excesses under Constantine that I have related above, and Christianity was still influenced by the Holy Spirit rather than man. At the end of the century an important event took place when a boy called Succat, who was being brought up in a Christian home, was kidnapped by Irish pirates and sold in Ireland to a minor chieftain. When he was sixteen, while looking after his pigs, he had a Holy Spirit conversion experience. Succat was later rescued, but while with his family again he knew God was telling him to return to Ireland and so he returned and, known later as Patrick, he converted many through the power of the Holy Spirit.

In the fifth century the barbarian hordes from Scandinavia and Europe swarmed into England; Christianity was driven out and the Dark Ages began. Christianity was pushed back, but it remained in Wales and in Ireland and in around 563 a man called Columba came from a church in Ireland that was founded by Patrick, to Iona in Scotland. Columba and his followers spread the Word and the Holy Spirit throughout Scotland and into northern England. This was not Roman Catholicism (the sacerdotal elements were hardly visible at that time) it was far more akin to the Christianity of the first two centuries than to what had developed since. The missionary fire that came out of Iona was also in Bangor in County Down, and from these places men with the fire of God in them travelled to central Europe and made a huge impact in that area. Sadly, their work in England was relatively ineffectual with the Saxons refusing to listen to the truth that was spoken to them. J H Merle d'Aubigne points out the danger of this in his classic 'The Reformation in England', Volume I:

'By neglecting this field, the Britons left room for other workmen, and thus it was that England left room for other workmen, and thus it was that England yielded to a foreign power, beneath its heavy yoke it long groaned in vain.' (page 33)

In 596 Gregory, Bishop of Rome, sent a prior called Augustine to Kent with the purpose of bringing the independent Church of Britain under the heel of Rome. Augustine and his team were accepted by the King of Kent and he made his headquarters in Canterbury. In 601 Augustine convened a council of British and Saxon Bishops near Worcester and demanded that the British Bishops recognise the authority of Rome, but they refused.

Sometime after the death of Augustine, Oswald, King of Northumbria, escaped political problems by fleeing to Scotland where he was converted. In 633 he returned at the head of a small army, and after prayer he had victory. Oswald asked for help from the monastery at Iona and several missionaries came from Scotland and Ireland to help him convert his people. The Word of God went into the south as well, but Oswald whilst still a young man, was killed in battle. Oswald was succeeded by Oswiu, a nominal Christian married to a Roman Catholic. His wife sent a young man called Wilfred to Rome to find out what Christianity was all about there and he returned a vigorous supporter of the

Pope. From then on there was much political activity in Oswiu's court to try to turn Northumbria to the Church of Rome. In 664 Wilfred felt the time was right to make a move and under the pretext of settling some disputes, particularly the date of Easter, he persuaded Oswiu to hold a Synod of Bishops at a monastery in Whitby. As d'Aubigne puts it:

'It was not a mere question about Easter, or certain rules of discipline, but of the great doctrine of the freedom of the church under Jesus Christ, or its enslavement under the papacy.' (page 47)

Unfortunately, the worldly wiles of Wilfred and his allies were no match for the politically naïve Colman who spoke for freedom and Oswiu fully embraced Rome. Had the decision gone the other way England and Scotland would probably have had a Church that taught biblical truths and moved in the power of the Holy Spirit and who knows where our history would have taken us.

The Reformation

From 793 for the next few hundred years Britain was beset by attacks from the Vikings. Their first reversal was at the battle of Ashdown in 871 when Ethelred and his two sons (one of whom was Alfred) defeated the Vikings. Alfred was a Christian and from his base in Winchester he did much to push back the influence of the Vikings and to spread Christianity. Alfred died in 899 and his descendants ruled for the first time over a united England.

To give an understanding of the state of the Church in England during the years leading up to the Reformation; in 1164 the king was informed by judges that in the last eight years 100 people had been murdered by churchmen. In 1213 King John made the monarchy a vassal of the Pope and in 1235 the Pope ordered the bishops in England to find Church offices for 300 Romans, including a place as Canon in Lincoln Cathedral for his infant nephew. The next three hundred years saw the monarchy trying to wrestle back its independence from the Pope. Monks, particularly the Franciscans, went about demanding money and telling people that they should give money to the church before giving money to the poor, and yet they lived in incredible opulence. Some monks would have lived a life of chastity and poverty, but the more that time went on, the less likely that this would have been the case. The Word of God was seldom spoken with any accuracy. In fact, many of the clergy were so badly educated that they preached about stories and myths rather than the Word of God and, to make matters worse, the laity was banned from reading the Bible. By the beginning of the sixteenth century many of the bishops were foreigners living abroad, and a large proportion of English wealth was going to the Pope and his cronies.

A similar picture could be seen across Europe, and so it was time for a change.

The Reformation in England

a) The reign of Henry VIII

The first signs of the Reformation in England came through the hands of the Dutchman Erasmus, who was living in England when his Greek and revised Latin New Testaments were published in 1516. Never before had a Greek, New Testament been published, nor one in Latin since the Vulgate early in the fourth century. In a letter Erasmus gave his reasons for publishing these books:

'The Holy Scriptures, translated into all languages, should be read not only by the Scottish and Irish, but even by Turks and Saracens. The husbandman should sing them as he holds the handle of his plough, the weaver repeat them as he plies his shuttle, and the wearied traveller, halting on his journey, refresh himself under some shady tree by these godly narratives.'

The publication of these books caused a huge storm in England, one completely unexpected by Erasmus. The Church saw the danger that these books could just be a precursor to the Bible in English, so set out to stir people up against these new translations. These books were very widely read by the educated in the land. Up until now few people were able to get hold of a Bible to read, this was partly due to the expense as before the invention of the printing press they were hand written, and partly because the Church discouraged the reading of the Bible. Of course, the Church's fears were proved justifiable, as the educated were able to see that what was in the Word of God was very different to what the Church had taught over the centuries. The Reformation had begun, with many coming to Christ through reading the New Testaments. Several of these converts were to play an important part in the fight against the King and the Church in the coming years, with some of them becoming martyrs. Oxford and Cambridge were the main places where eyes were opened at this time.

One of those who were awakened in Oxford was William Tyndale, who also was to die a martyr, but not before he had brought into the world an English version of the New Testament and much of the Old. About 80% of the King James Bible comes from Tyndale's translation. This extraordinary man, who had an incredible gift for languages, enabled the ordinary British man and woman to read the Word of God. It was reported in Foxe's Book of Martyrs that one day Tyndale had a discussion with a learned man who was getting the worse of the discussion and said, *'We were better be without God's laws than the pope's;'* to which Tyndale replied, *'If God spare my life ere many years, I will cause a boy that driveth the plough, shall know more of the scripture than thou dost.'* He succeeded in doing this. In England, more than anywhere else, it was a Reformation of the Word. When men and women read the New Testament in English, the Holy Spirit opened their eyes to see the rottenness of the Church and the lies they had been told.

By 1521 the translated works of the German monk, Martin Luther, were flooding into England. Luther is considered the father of the Reformation and he advocated a split from the Pope, rejection of tradition and a return to the principles of the New Testament. His ideas were quickly picked up by others in Northern Europe. Luther's works were widely read, but in 1521 the Church banned all his books and King Henry VIII wrote a paper in support of the Pope and against Luther. For this work the Pope made the King *'Defender of the Faith'*, a title the Queen still holds today.

These next years were ones where the Reformation struggled to gain a foothold as the Church succeeded in persecuting those who were supporting it. In 1526 Tyndale's New Testament in English, which was written on the continent, was smuggled into London. The Church was determined to stop Tyndale's Testament, so they hunted down those who were selling it and those who had bought it. Several became martyrs; the young men of Oxford and Cambridge suffered most.

Henry's desire to have a male heir brought him to seek a divorce from his Spanish wife, Catherine. Only the Pope could authorise the divorce, but he was more afraid of the Holy Roman Emperor, who was Catherine's nephew, than he was of Henry. In 1529 Henry was introduced to the idea of splitting from Rome and taking back the lordship of his kingdom that had been given up three hundred years earlier. Henry really liked this idea of being an independent king, free from the political and financial constraints imposed on him by being a vassal to the Pope.

In November 1529 Henry called the first Parliament for seven years and this Parliament prepared to attack the numerous abuses of the Church. The members of the Commons were no doubt influenced by Erasmus' and Tyndale's Testaments and the works of Luther, so the time was right for a change. The Church, fearful of what they might do, tried to pre-empt them by making some changes themselves. They declared that priests should no longer keep shops or taverns, not play dice and not hunt with dogs and birds. The Commons went further; making laws against the fees paid to the Church on wills etc, against clergy holding more than one post, against holding a post while living somewhere else, and against holding secular jobs.

This was a start, it was the first time the laity had victory over the clergy. Although Henry was prepared to break from Rome, he was not prepared to allow the English Bible into England, so persecution remained. Like Constantine, Henry wanted unity of doctrine in his kingdom, so he would not give in to the reformers in order to prevent a great division between Catholics and Protestants. Also, like Constantine, Henry wanted to be in control of the Church himself and to do this he needed to get out from under the authority of Rome and reduce the power of the clergy.

In 1531 the king was informed of an old statute that showed that the clergy had broken the law by accepting the appointment of a papal legate in the English Church. This was clearly ridiculous because Henry had told them to accept him, but technically they had all broken the law. This gave the king the excuse he needed, so he demanded a £100,000 fine and the Church's acknowledgement that he was head of the Church rather than the Pope. The clergy hated this, but after heated discussions they agreed.

Henry needed the bishops against the Pope, and the bishops needed the king against the heretics, and so the king supported the clergy and persecutions increased. In 1532 Henry forced the Church to give up their power of independent legislation and their oath of allegiance to the Pope, and he stopped payments made to the Pope by the bishops on their appointment. Henry was determined to substitute himself for the Pope and yet keep the country away from Protestantism. He was taking Rome out of Roman Catholicism, so he persecuted both the papists and the reformers. In 1534 Parliament prohibited all appeals to the Pope, and bishops were no longer to be appointed by him. On June 9th Henry abolished all the authority of the Pope in England.

In 1535/6 the abuses of the monasteries were dealt with through officials visiting each one and recording the abuses that took place there. The results of the enquiry confirmed what most had suspected, having recorded dreadful acts of licentiousness, greed and violence, the dissolution of the monasteries began in 1535, ending in 1539. Their wealth went to the crown.

In 1536 the reformers achieved a victory when permission was given to distribute the Bible in English. The Bible chosen was Coverdale's, as that of Tyndale had too much 'history' attached to it. Despite tending to favour the Roman Catholic party, on September 5th, 1538 Henry surprised everyone when he decreed that every church should have a Bible in English and that the people should be encouraged to read it. This time it was a new edition of Tyndale's Bible. Together with this decree there were others; to turn away from objects of superstition and idolatry and to not give money to images and relics.

Until Henry's death in 1547 there was a constant attempt by the Catholic party to try to get back to the way things were and to stop the advancement of the reformers. The king tried to keep a balance between the two and would equally persecute both sides. However, at the end of his reign, apart from the break with Rome, a cleaning up of the Church abuses, the dissolution of the monasteries and the English Bible in every church, not a lot had changed. One would probably call the Church very high Anglo-Catholic at this time and there was still plenty that the reformers wanted to change.

b)   The reign of Edward VI

The Earl of Hertford, soon to become Duke of Somerset, seized control of the country by making himself Protector of the young king Edward VI. Somerset was a Protestant, and in 1547 he ordered a set of sermons to be put in the churches, and that both the bread and the wine be administered to the congregation. In 1548 some churches in London were allowed to have all their services in English and all images were removed from churches. By 1549 the English Prayer Book was adopted as the only legal form of worship, which to a large degree was a compromise, as a significant amount of the old Mass was retained.

In 1549 Somerset fell and the Duke of Northumberland took over, continuing the Reformation. In 1550 he gave instructions that priests should preach the Word rather than celebrate Mass, altars were to be replaced with a table and the lifting up of the wafer in adoration as well as medieval vestments, were banned. In 1552 came Cranmer's second Prayer Book, which is the basis for the Prayer Book still in use today in the Anglican Church. In the Communion service Cranmer tried to ensure that everything included was scriptural.

In 1553 Edward died, leaving a much reformed Church with all signs of the papacy gone. The Mass was gone and the Anglican Church looked a good deal the way it does today.

c)   The reign of Mary

Mary was on the throne for five years and is remembered for the burnings of Protestants on her way to restoring Catholicism in England. She did everything she could to reverse what had gone before, but this is not relevant to what we are studying, as Elizabeth just reversed everything again once she was Queen. One aspect of Mary's reign was important, though, and that was her burnings forced several Protestants to flee the country for Germany and Switzerland.

Following Luther's stand against Rome other leaders rose up to follow him. Zwingli was one and he was based in Zurich. An attempt was made to unite Zwingli and Luther, but this proved impossible as Zwingli believed that the bread and the wine merely represented the body and blood of Christ, whereas Luther believed that Christ was present in some way in the bread and wine, although he did not believe that they were the actual body and blood of Christ the way the Catholics did. Bucer was another leader and he agreed with much of what Zwingli said, although he opposed Zwingli's belief that Church and State should be merged. Bucer was invited to live in England by Cranmer and his views influenced many.

Perhaps the reformer who had greatest influence in England was Calvin, who was based in Geneva. It was not surprising therefore that the exiles congregated in Switzerland and Germany. John Fox reported in his famous 'Book of Martyrs' that there were 800 exiles, and he should know as he was one of them. Although this does not sound like many, several of them were to have important positions in England under Elizabeth. According to A G Dickens in his book 'The English Reformation':

'More important, the exiled clergy, so far from being ordinary parish priests,

111

included the leading figures among the Protestant scholars of both universities, many of whom were to achieve bishoprics and other high offices in the Elizabethan Church.'

There were around 200 exiles based in Geneva and these experienced the fullness of Calvin's version of Church Government. Like many others Calvin wanted to get back to the Church of the New Testament, so his church had no episcopacy, it had congregational singing without instruments, psalms instead of hymns and there was an element of democracy. Some of this English group wanted to translate the Bible into English to more reflect the reformers' view, so in 1557 they produced a New Testament; this was followed in 1560 by the whole Bible with critical notes which became known as the 'Geneva Bible'. This Bible became very popular and was the most used Bible until the KJV, which was produced to nullify the Puritanical teachings that could be found in the notes of the Geneva Bible (as mentioned in chapter 3), eventually replacing it. There were around 140 editions before the Geneva Bible became unfashionable in the mid-seventeen century.

d)   The reign of Elizabeth I

There is evidence to suggest that Elizabeth leaned more towards the Church of her father Henry than to that wanted by the more extreme reformers such as those exiles in Geneva, but that was probably more to do with politics than with any faith Elizabeth may have had. However, the Parliament of 1559 would not accept the cautious approach of the Queen. Many of the exiles had returned and a dozen or more were elected to that Parliament and they had a considerable influence over the mood of the other members. The noticeable absentees were the leaders of the exiles in Geneva who delayed their return, an action that may have had a significant effect on the structure of the Elizabethan Church as those in Parliament at this time, although Protestants were moderates.

Many of the exiles would have been very disappointed with the results of this important Parliament as, far from taking the Reformation forward from the position held at the end of Edward VI's reign, it actually took a step backwards. Because Elizabeth wanted to be more moderate the 1552 Prayer Book was accepted, albeit with some changes. The Queen, wanting to help Catholics accept the Prayer Book, added to the words spoken at Communion, 'The body of our Lord Jesus Christ, which was given for you....,' which hinted at transubstantiation if you wanted to read that into the words. Another change was one that brought ornaments back into the church and compelled the clergy to wear vestments again. This was very unpopular and several clergy refused to wear their vestments, resulting in some being deprived of their livings.

In 1563 the 39 Articles were established by the Church. These Articles repudiated the Catholic ideas of transubstantiation and the Mass and set out the basis of Anglican faith. Elizabeth made sure that they were wide enough to include various shades of Protestantism and that people knew that she was head of the Church. Just like Constantine and her father, she had to have a State Church that was uniform across the country and under her control. From 1563 until the present day the Anglican Church has not changed very much. It still has the 1552 Prayer Book, although it was revised in 1662, and it still has the 39 Articles. In 1559 Elizabeth was trying to create a structure in which people of varying religious hues, from Catholic to Puritan, could exist under one roof. One has to say that she succeeded in part because, despite tensions, the Anglican Church today includes Anglo-Catholics, Evangelicals, Charismatics and Liberals. Whether this is a good thing or not is open to debate.

Summary

So by the end of the sixteenth century there was a compromise Church established that had thrown out the excesses of the Catholics, but had not embraced fully the teachings of Luther and Calvin. Many Protestants were unhappy with the Settlement, wanting changes in the liturgy and ceremonial; particularly as far as Catholic tradition was concerned. The Marian exiles had spent five years in the heartland of the reformers and many returned to England with new thoughts on how the Church should look; these men and women were called Puritans. The word 'puritan' came to be used as a form of abuse during the reign of Mary, but now tended to mean someone who wanted to simplify forms of worship and who wanted to model the Church more on the lines of the New Testament Church.

There were five main points advocated by Luther, Calvin and the other reformers:

1) The Mass. The Eucharist was replaced as the central point of the service with the sermon, and this was taken up by the Anglican Church as well. The sermon had lost its place in worship many centuries before, but it is still the predominant part of the worship service today in Protestant churches.

2) The Priesthood of all Believers. The reformers believed that we are all priests and we can all have direct communion with God; we did not need the priest as a mediator. Linked to this concept was the belief that there was no difference between clergy and laity and we could all interpret the Word of God. If there was no difference between clergy and laity then episcopacy would have to go. None of the English monarchs would accept this idea, so the churches maintained very much a sense of 'them and us' which we still have today in the Anglican and many other churches.

Although the reformers generally believed that we can all approach God directly, that we are all ministers, and that we all have a divine calling, they do not seem to have taken that further and encouraged us to minister to those outside the church building. The calling they believed in seems to be a secular one rather than a spiritual one. Maybe this did not occur to them because the members of the congregations did not appear to be active in the spiritual gifts. Calvin believed that apostles and prophets were only for New Testament times and evangelists were only raised up in places where religion had fallen into decay, but that pastors and teachers were permanent, so he could not have believed in equipping the saints in the prophetic, evangelism etc. The equipping was for us to lead better Christian lives and not to change society.

3) Justification by faith, which was accepted by all parties.

4) The authority of the Scriptures over all of man's ideas, which was also accepted by all.

5) That the bread and the wine both be administered at communion was also accepted by all. Although all rejected transubstantiation, Luther had a slightly different view compared with the rest who took the bread and the wine as representative of the body and blood of Christ.

The Elizabethan Settlement enabled Catholics and Puritans to co-exist, even though neither was very happy about it. Despite the Queen's inclination to resist changes suggested by the Puritans, the reformed religion spread around the kingdom. As already noted, many of the exiles were well placed in Elizabeth's government and most of the important bishops early in her reign were Puritans. The majority of the Puritans had been influenced by Calvin's teachings rather than Luther's, as the Lutheran states had tended to be isolationist, whereas Switzerland welcomed those wanting to learn. Cambridge was a hotbed for Calvinism and many of the new clerics who came out of that city were Puritans who took up posts all over the kingdom.

It just shows the power of teaching - theological colleges today produce pastors who reflect the views of their teachers. Jack Deere is a good example; he used to teach at a seminary in America that the gifts of the Spirit were for apostolic times only; they were not relevant any more. He then received a major touch of the Holy Spirit that transformed his teaching. Thank goodness he received the correct revelation, but how many teachers are out there who are not teaching truth and their students are not checking for themselves the truth of the teaching?

A compromise can never work for long as those on the extremes will eventually break out. Elizabeth's compromise worked for a while, in fact for most of her reign, but there was a cost: persecution. In order to control the doctrine of the Church Elizabeth had to make the penalties heavy for not conforming. A lecturer at Cambridge at that time was Thomas Cartwright, who said that Church should be organised on the basis of what it says in the 'Acts of the Apostles' and that Calvin's church in Geneva was a good model. He was strongly against the episcopacy because it could not be found in the New Testament Church, and because of his opposition, he was imprisoned several times. Cartwright often went into exile to avoid prison. He is considered to be the first Presbyterian. He died in 1603 and his ideas were later taken up by many in the seventeenth century.

Another 'rebel' was Robert Browne who was influenced by the teachings of Cartwright when he was at Cambridge. Browne wanted separation from the Anglican Church, he rejected it as unscriptural and it was only his high family connections that prevented him from long imprisonment or even execution. He is called a Separatist, or an Independent, but he is also considered the first Congregationalist. He died in 1633. Less fortunate were John Copping, Elias Thacker, Henry Barrow, John Greenwood and John Penry who were all hanged for being Separatists. What I find telling is that, even in the glorious Elizabethan age, these men were executed for having views little different to the ones I am expressing in this book.

Most Puritans were able to live under the Elizabethan Settlement mainly because there were so many pastors and bishops who were sympathetic to their beliefs, and so long as they did not try to form a separate Church, the Queen would leave them alone. However, this all changed in the next century under James I and Charles I when the leading bishops and the monarch thought that they needed to suppress the Puritans, whether they were part of the Anglican Church or not. They did not understand how many people held these views. When Parliament was called it was full of people who were either Puritan or against Catholicism. When faced with persecution and with the concern that

Catholicism was creeping back, they rose up and kicked Charles I off the throne. There were additional reasons for the start of the Civil War, but this was a significant one.

Many denominations and sects were birthed in the period between 1555 and 1640. Presbyterianism, Congregationalism, Lutheranism, Baptists, Independents etc. Once the people were able to read the Bible it was impossible to keep everyone under the control of one doctrine; new denominations were bound to form and most of them were just trying to get to a form of Church that was closer to the biblical model. People could see that the Anglican Church was still burdened with tradition, and they realised that some of what was in the Prayer Book and some of what they could see in the churches was not biblical. There were still vestments, incense, processions, images, altar rails etc and above all there was episcopacy.

CHAPTER 7

What is hindering your stepping out?

We have looked at the changing Church up to the death of Elizabeth I in 1603. To a large extent the Church today is much the same as it was in 1603 just with greater variety. It does not matter where you have come from in the world; your church has the same roots as ours. The Anglican Church has more flexibility in that it covers a wide spectrum from almost Catholic to almost Puritan and from Conservative to Liberal. However, the Church has split into many more denominations than there were in 1603. As explained, several appeared in the seventeenth century, and then the Methodists appeared in the eighteenth century, the Pentecostals at the start of the twentieth and the house church movement in the second half of the twentieth century.

So generally speaking, most of the churches in the United Kingdom today are similar; they generally meet in a building, they generally have a pastor and their services mostly have similar components. It is my contention that the Church is generally not fit for purpose. The past has become a hindrance to our moving into a new wineskin. The Church's purpose is to help draw people closer to God through worship, to help the encouragement of one another through love, and to bring about the equipping and the releasing of the saints. Please understand that I am not trying to rubbish all churches and all pastors, I just want you to see what might be holding you and others back from achieving your destiny. You can see that Church today is completely different from that of the New Testament, and some people believe that we must get the Church back to the way it was in the first century by abolishing all church buildings and returning to church in the home. However, I believe that we have thousands of church buildings and thousands of pastors in the United Kingdom and God has often used them powerfully in the past, despite their imperfections. We just have to make some changes that make the Church more fit for purpose. We do not want to go back to the past; we want to look to what God wants to do in the future.

The Lord is looking for a new wineskin (Matthew 9:17) in order to release the saints (all of us) to step out and fulfil the Great Commission. I want to highlight some issues in the Church that might be hindering your stepping out in what God has called you to do, and make some suggestions as to how the Church might change so that it might become the new wineskin. I pray that the Holy Spirit will open your eyes and understanding.

Tradition

You have probably heard this story. A teenager is sitting down to roast beef for Sunday lunch with her family. She says 'Mum, why do you cut the ends off the beef and put them on top of the joint?' Her mother replied 'Darling, it is the way we have always done it; ask your grandmother.' So next time she saw her grandmother she asked the same question and her grandmother replied 'Surely your mother does not still do that? I used to do it because my oven was too small for the joint!'

Tradition is often something we do because we have always done it, but we don't know why we are doing it. The Reformation was much about investigating what had been done for centuries in the Church and seeing if it appeared in the New Testament, and they found that much of what they did could not be supported by Scripture. This was because people had often merged their Greek heritage with their Christian beliefs and come up with something that was not truth. Jesus made his feelings clear in Matthew 15:3:

'Jesus replied, "And why do you break the command of God for the sake of your tradition?"'

We must ensure that we go back to the Word of God and not the traditions of man. I recently received a report of a theological discussion on an issue between half a dozen leaders who I highly respect. One of them said 'it will undo 1700 years of Church history,' referring to if a particular view was adopted. You will notice that 1700 years takes us back to Constantine and not Jesus; he was saying that 1700 years of the opinion of man will be undone.

Tradition can be 1700 years old or 20; most of us look upon something in our upbringing as tradition. I grew up as a nominal Christian, going to church several times a week while I was at school. I became used to the organ music and singing hymns; I felt comfortable with them, they became traditional. I became a Christian in a church that had bands and choruses and it took me some time to embrace that form of worship; for a long time I wanted to sing hymns because that was what I was used to. I felt uncomfortable singing choruses, and even walked out of church when the worship began and walked around the square outside until it was over. After a while I forced myself to participate and now I just love that form of music.

I was comfortable in my tradition; holding on to tradition stops people from moving on. The Lord used William Haslam to bring revival to Norfolk in 1872. A Rector's wife wrote to him saying that she and her husband had been praying for revival in Norfolk for years, but 'if this is a revival, it has come in such a way that I cannot thank God for it.' Revival had come in a way that was not how she traditionally thought revival should come, so she was willing to reject this wonderful move of God because it came in a new way. Just as with me, her views on what was traditional stopped her moving on. It is said that the first into one move of God is the last into the next. This is because people think that they have the answers for God used them in a particular way last time, but God never does anything in the same way, so unless we die to our traditions, it will be very difficult for us to recognise the next move of God. The ultimate example of this was Jesus. The religious leaders in Jesus' day were not expecting a carpenter to be the Messiah; Jesus did not fit in with the traditional view of what the Messiah would look like.

I spoke to a Catholic to try to understand how they view tradition. She made a good point that by sticking to tradition there is a great sense of unity in the Catholic Church because you can go practically anywhere in the world and the service will be the same. She said that she really enjoyed the liturgy, but even she found that sometimes, by repeating things so many times, she forgot the meaning behind her responses.

We should always be checking what we do in church and in our every day lives to ensure that it is part of God's plan and purpose for our lives. As we have already seen the Anglican Church service is still based on the 1552 Prayer Book, but was that truth for then, and is it truth today? Great intellectuals have said it is right to use the Prayer Book, but is it? I am not saying it isn't right, I am just saying that there should be no 'sacred cows,' everything must be open to regular re-evaluation. I believe that we should look at everything we do in church and we should check everything that is in and around the church building to make sure that it is helping us, or at least not hindering us in making the church fit for purpose. There are many things we do in church that seem a good idea at a micro level, but I encourage you to always think about how any change will affect God's overall plan. We must not put God in a box; we must always be flexible to bend, to change and to adapt to whatever God is saying now. If we want to move into the new things that God has for us, we need to re-evaluate our traditions.

Individualism

I have to admit that individualism is something I had never heard of until recently. In 2006 I was having some counselling and the couple praying for me mentioned that I was an individualist. I thought that they were complimenting me and I proudly agreed with them. I told them that it had stood me in good stead over the years in my role as a consultant and in what I do in the Body of Christ. It was only in my final session, when they said that they were going to pray my individualism off me, that I realised that they were not being complimentary. I was aghast and quickly told them that I was quite happy being an individualist, thank you. I had visions of many of my giftings disappearing and my not being able to do the things I thought I was good at. It was only during the research of this book that I began to realise how much of a problem it is in the Church, and I suppose someday I shall have to go back to receive more prayer.

We have already seen how the New Testament Church was full of love and community, with everyone sharing what they had and supporting one another. They lived out the biblical teaching of each person being part of a Body, depending on one another and working together for their mutual edification. They understood Jesus' command was for us to love one another:

'A new command I give you: Love one another. As I have loved you, so you must love one another.' (John 13:34)

Anything that God calls us to do will inevitably involve showing love to someone. So what has happened to the love that was experienced in the early Church? For my first eight years as a Christian, I went to what many would call a good church; it was growing and I heard several people say that it was like coming home when they found us for the first time. The people were friendly when you arrived on Sunday and we chatted merrily after the service at the back of the church; however, I often left the church on Sunday feeling lonely. I had quite a high profile in the church, as I was always doing something there, but in all those eight years I can honestly remember only one or two close friends, the pastor and one other person, invite me to Sunday lunch in their homes.

I don't think that I am the only person to experience this. In fact, a close friend of mine began a ministry where every month she asked a family to host Sunday lunch in her home and she invited six or eight single people to join them. That was a really worthwhile ministry and many lonely people were encouraged and built up. For those in loving families it really does not cost much to add one or two more people to the family Sunday lunch. With the breakdown of the family in our society, this form of ministry would bring a tremendous blessing to all concerned.

The Reformation took the Church from one extreme to the other. The Church of the Middle Ages was generally one of community in that everyone went to church, and because it was difficult to travel very far in those days, everyone lived close by. This meant that people would not only go to church on Sunday, but they would relate to one another all week in their work, shopping and socialising. However, the Church of that period had become a sick institution. As a reaction to the control and abuse of the Church, the reformers taught that the individual had direct access to God and that all one really needed was your Bible. Jordan Bajis discusses Individualism more fully in chapter 11 of his book 'Common Ground'; in it he says:

'The "church" here (on the earth) came to be seen as a beachhead from which people could be evangelized into the "heavenly church," and as a classroom where "personal" holiness could be taught; only secondarily was it an environment of relationships. Fellowship with Christians was "nice," but it certainly wasn't necessary for godliness or instruction in the Christian life, nor was it a requirement for Christian service.'

It is much more difficult these days to be a community because very few people who meet together on Sunday have any connection during the week with regards to work and shopping. However, clearly the biggest problem to our spending time with one another is the busy lives we lead. How many times have you heard people use busyness as an excuse for not getting together with you? This is something that must be addressed in the Body of Christ; it is ungodly. We have to realise the importance of our having our lives in balance, so many of us need to make changes to our lifestyles. Somehow we have come to believe that we must work to create a wonderful lifestyle for our spouse and children, so we buy the most expensive house we can afford, with the largest mortgage the bank will give, and then we spend the rest of our lives working all hours in order to keep the house. After a few years we are doing quite well, so of course we need a bigger house and we can now afford a bigger mortgage, so we upgrade. We are never satisfied, we have to go higher and higher, and the result is that work replaces God, the family, and time with the Lord and with the children disappears into nothingness. How can we change society if we live in this ungodly way?

We live in a society where there is family breakdown and where we live isolated lives with no feeling of responsibility to anyone. Sadly, this is true in

Church as well as outside it.

'The entire law is summed up in a single command: "Love your neighbour as yourself."' (Galatians 5:14)

The phrase 'Love your neighbour as yourself' appears ten times in the Bible and it is a very emphatic statement that brooks no flexibility of understanding. Our first purpose in life is to love God and then to love our neighbour; we do this through interaction with people in our daily lives and in whatever work the Lord has called us to do. After GOD and neighbour comes family and work; we desperately need to understand this and change our lifestyles accordingly. The situation is not helped by the ungodly demands to do overtime at work, but we have to realise what these demands are doing to our relationship with God, to what God has called us to do, to our health and to our families. How can you hear God tell you about your calling if you are in this merry-go-round, and how on earth do you find the time to fulfil it?

Individualism has grown in the West over the centuries and is one of the main problems that prevent us from stepping out in our calling. It is not our fault, it is what we have been taught, it is ingrained into us as children; but once we recognise the problem we have a responsibility to change. The breakdown of the family unit forces us to depend on ourselves and not others. Those of us who went to boarding school had it drummed into us that we need to stand on our own two feet; our society values individual achievement in sports and business; we honour beautiful people who lead giddy hedonistic lifestyles and the government encourages single parenting and alternative lifestyles over family. Individualism has become a curse over our nation; we have to change our mindsets and learn more about community, fellowship and love.

Church

We have already touched on several of the points I am going to mention here, but let us look at how they affect us today.

125

a)   The building

If we look at the traditional church building we see a great stone edifice with high ceilings, big arches, stained glass windows, maybe a balcony; all of which create an atmosphere of awe and reverence. Many have tiled floors that are not only cold in temperature, but they leave one cold spiritually. Some people I know do get something spiritual from the grandness of buildings, but does this help in creating an atmosphere of love and encouragement?

Many traditional churches still have pews, which in my opinion do nothing to promote a family environment and a sense of togetherness. In years gone by some pews were like boxes and some were so high that the preacher could not see the people inside. Whether pews or chairs they all face the altar and for me they give a sense of aloneness; you just see the pastor and the back of someone's head, again there is no sense of togetherness. Then you have the pulpit, raised floor or platform from which the pastor addresses you and gives his sermon. This part of the church is specifically designed, especially the pulpit, to give the pastor a sense of power and control over the congregation, and the congregation a sense of respect and obedience. In Pentecostal churches the pastor is often seated on the platform, another device to show how superior the pastor is in spiritual matters. Most church buildings, traditional or otherwise, are laid out to show the congregation the special status of the pastor; little has changed since the days of Constantine's basilicas. The traditional church building, particularly, but also many other churches, reinforce the clergy-laity divide which hinders the doctrine of the 'Priesthood of all Believers' and the releasing of the saints into works of service.

Some traditional churches have made some positive moves by putting in chairs instead of pews, covering the tiles with a carpet, not using the pulpit and creating a 'coffee' area at the back etc. However, some churches hang on to their pews for dear life. I have suggested to one or two people that perhaps chairs would give them more flexibility and you should have seen their faces! Many people see pews as part of what they have always understood to be

Church; it is as if they felt that without pews and cold floors there could be no church. It is interesting to note that before pews people used to stand.

A carpet and chairs do help to make the space more flexible and more conducive to creating a family environment where people can love and encourage one another, but it is difficult to get over the cold, reverential atmosphere that the building is designed to create. The early Church was warm and joyful and it is difficult to recreate this in a traditional building.

b)   The sung worship

There are two main types of sung worship in the Church. One is still with the organ, and maybe a choir; the other is with a band. I am also going to include dancing here. Whether the singing is hymns or choruses does not matter, because everyone is different in the way they like to express their worship to the Lord. The problems I have here are with the danger of the congregation focusing on the band rather than the Lord, and the fact that specialist musicians tend to prevent some of the congregation exercising their gifts in this area.

In churches that have bands I have come across many instances of people becoming the centre of attention rather than Christ. To begin with the band is nearly always on a platform at the front so that you see them high and lifted up when you are worshipping. I visit a number of churches and I sometimes get the impression that the band are giving more of a performance at a concert than leading people into the presence of God. This sense of 'performance' is a natural problem to occur as they are on a platform, just like in a theatre, and there is a danger of pride entering in, especially for the leader.

We have seen in the early Church that the worshippers would be led by the Holy Spirit; someone would lead in singing a psalm and then another would start a spiritual song, and people would play different musical instruments from time to time. Having 'professional' musicians in the church does tend to take away the opportunity for people to exercise their giftings and for the Holy Spirit to do what He wants. The songs are all prepared beforehand and the congregation have to sing whatever the worship leader has chosen. The spontaneity of the Holy Spirit is not really allowed. Sometimes there is a space for singing in tongues, but sometimes I wonder if the Holy Spirit prompted the worship leader to stop or if he always stopped after that particular time in the service.

Dancing as an expression of worship is a lovely thing, but it does tend to reinforce the individualism that is in the church. The dancing in the early Church was most likely group dancing in circles such as can be seen in Messianic gatherings. One sees dancing in very few churches, although it is becoming more popular. In traditional churches with pews there is normally no area for people to dance, but elsewhere it should be no problem and I wish more people did it.

There can, however, be problems associated with worship dancing; one is pride that allows people's focus to wander from the Lord onto a dancer. For this reason I would have dancing at the side or back of the church. Dancing can also become a performance; in one church I have been to there was a raised part of the platform particularly for three dancers who wore special clothing. This was raising up these young women as special, and people tended to focus their attention on them while they danced. In my opinion there is a place for a performance of dancing on special occasions, but not as a regular part of the service.

Personally I would like to see more group dancing in churches because it involves mutual participation which is more in line with the early Church. If we were to have more freedom of expression in worship, through singing and dancing, then I believe that our relationship with the Lord and with one another would benefit.

c)   The pastor

Historically, what do most pastors do in the church? I am focusing here on churches of less than 200 people because churches bigger than that will often have more than one pastor. Remember, I am generalising here, but in a Sunday service the pastor will probably give a welcome, give the sermon, give communion and close the service. He/she may also say the prayers and read the lesson, but members of the congregation may do this. The pastor will also visit the elderly and the sick, do baptisms, marriages and funerals, deal with people's problems, look after the vision of the church, watch over the staff, prepare the sermon, spend time with the Lord and then he has his family and friends. I wish I could understand how he copes with all this.

The reformers believed in the 'priesthood of all believers', but they still had the pastor/teacher do everything, so as far as the congregation was concerned nothing had really changed; they were not allowed to do the work of priests. Luther did have a problem here, in that the average person who attended church was uneducated and had been kept in the dark regarding biblical truths for generations, so the practicalities of releasing such people into ministries may have been the reason why he did not activate the 'priesthood of all believers' doctrine. So for 1,700 or 1,800 years the congregation has sat in church and their maximum contribution has been to sing songs they are told to sing; say amen at the end of some prayers or a reading and maybe recite the Lord's Prayer or a Creed. We have already seen how the church building is created to emphasise the separation of clergy and laity and the role of the pastor does exactly the same thing. The building and pastor create an environment where the members of the congregation come to accept that they have no role in the service and that the pastor does everything, and they just have to open their ears and listen. Luther said *'the ears are the only organs of a Christian'*. No wonder the Church changed little in the Reformation. Many pastors do get some people to help serve the tea, hand out programmes, welcome people etc but these are all services to the church. In the traditional church environment it is difficult to create an atmosphere where people can be equipped and envisioned to heal the sick, drive out demons, raise the dead etc.

The Reformation helped Christians to understand the truths of the Bible that had been hidden for centuries, but it did nothing to help Christians become ministers. We need a new Reformation to bring the Church into its biblical role. In recent years some pastors have begun to realise that their role is not to do everything and I shall discuss this more in the next chapter.

d)　The service

Virtually all churches have an order of service that is the same each week. How therefore, can the Holy Spirit do what he wants to do in the service? I have occasionally seen the pastor give in to the Holy Spirit and just allow Him to do what He wants, but this is incredibly rare and the times I have seen it have mostly been at conferences. A few friends have told me that their pastor allows the Holy Spirit free reign, but this is not the norm.

Apart from the reasons already given as to why we are in church, something that overrides these is the will of God. Our overwhelming desire must be to bring the Kingdom of Heaven down onto the earth, and our greatest wish is for the Presence of God to come in our midst, and this is only likely to happen when the service reflects God's will rather than our will. I do understand that an order of service gives some people a sense of security. It is comforting to know that whichever church you go to the order of service is likely to be roughly what one is used to, but is the purpose of church to make us feel comfortable and secure?

e)　The sermon

As already mentioned, the sermon is not biblical, but that is not to say it doesn't have some purpose. The sermon is generally given by the pastor and in a charismatic service it normally takes up about half the allotted time, although less time in a traditional service. Assuming that the sermon is mostly used as a tool to equip us for service, think about how many times in the last year you have been impacted by the sermon. Of course, your answer may vary according to how long you have been a Christian and the quality of teacher in your church. I recently asked 15 mature, passionate Christians I know from several different churches, who regularly attend church, and they replied 'on average' that they were impacted by a sermon four times in the last year. Now I know that 15 people are hardly a good sample, but I do believe that this highlights an issue that needs attention.

Another issue to consider is why the pastor must always be the one to give the sermon? There will always be some in the congregation who have a gift of teaching/preaching, so why are these people not given an opportunity to use their gifts? By tradition we always have a sermon. I remember in 1994, during the 'Toronto Blessing' outpouring, my pastor saying that we could not have a service without the Word being preached. My question is 'why not'? The answer is that Luther said that there could be no meeting without a sermon and prayers, so the sermon is in the service through the tradition of man.

The sermon also reinforces the clergy/laity divide in that it gives the impression that the pastor is the only person who knows enough, and is gifted enough, to teach the congregation. This also encourages passivity in the congregation.

Summary

The aspects of the Church that we have discussed make we wonder why we go to church each Sunday. If we are there to worship the Lord, how do we do this effectively when we have a fixed time for each part of the service and we are told what to sing and what to pray? Some churches have extended times of worship that I am sure are a blessing to the Lord but this is rare. Many people are able to worship the Lord more effectively at home, on their own, than in church.

Where and how do we engender love and encourage one another in church? About the only time we talk to one another in church is at the end of the service, and my experience is that on the whole you ask someone how they are and you get a 'fine' reply, even if the person has just been beaten up by her husband. Some people have a jolly time with their friends but that is not the point. The point is to show love towards those we don't know and the church building is not a good environment for this; even if it happens it is only at a superficial level as little can be achieved in ten minutes.

When do we get equipped for works of service? New Christians certainly get a lot out of the sermon, but this is normally equipping to lead a better life as a Christian. This is important so that we can be more like Jesus to our fellow man, but sermons are not used to help the saints identify their calling or to give them tools to carry it out.

In the next chapter we will look at suggestions for the Church so that it can better fulfil its purposes.

CHAPTER 8

How the Church can change

In the previous chapter I showed some reasons why the Church is falling short of its purpose with a result that we are not getting equipped and we are not changing society. In this chapter I am going to give some suggestions as to how the Church might change.

An important barrier to change is the inflexibility of the Church and its inability to see what God is doing. An example of this can be seen in its attitude towards revival. I believe that in the United Kingdom the great denominational churches such as the Anglicans, the Methodists and the Baptists have never been able to sustain revival. If we look at the Great Awakening (not to be confused with the US revival of the same period) of the eighteenth century we will find that John Wesley, although an ordained minister in the Anglican Church, was soon banned from preaching in most Anglican churches. At the same time in Wales there were several wonderful revivalist preachers who wanted to minister as Anglican priests but they were forbidden. Incredibly the revival led by Methodist Hugh Bourne less than twenty years after the death of John Wesley was not accepted by the Methodist Church, so Bourne and his followers were forced to form the Primitive Methodists. Fifty years later William Booth was moving in revival across England and again the Methodist Church could not accept it and he had to leave the Church. While a wonderful revival was happening under Booth's ministry in Cornwall, there was the annual Methodist meeting which coincidentally took place in Cornwall. They passed a motion at the meeting banning the use of Methodist churches by Booth, even though thousands were coming to the Lord through his meetings. Even the renewing move of the Holy Spirit that came from Toronto in 1994, having been initially embraced by parts of the Anglican Church, was eventually pushed out or suppressed by most of the churches. Today only a few churches are moving in the same power they moved in ten years ago. These are mainly non-denominational churches that are linked with the Toronto Airport Christian Fellowship.

As soon as a denomination forms it loses flexibility. Inevitably rules are put in place like the 1552 Prayer Book and the 39 Articles to distinguish a member of the denomination from someone else. If you do not conform to the rules then you are persecuted as the Protestants were by the Catholic Church and the Puritans by the Anglican Church. Now God never seems to come in the same way twice, so organisations that have rules that probably defined the way God came last time, cannot recognise Him coming in a new way. It is mainly to these denominational churches that I make my suggestions. It is vital that churches remain flexible and open to the Holy Spirit having His way, so that they can fulfil their purposes in equipping and releasing the saints.

For the last few years we have been in a new season, a new time. It is now the day of the saints and not the priests. It is the day of the individual believer changing society through their witness and signs and wonders; it is no longer the day of the superstar. It is a new time and therefore we need a new wineskin for God to fulfil His purposes. This requires the old wineskin to change and adapt, ever ready to react to the will of the Holy Spirit.

Home groups

The main differences between the New Testament Church and the Church today are its size and where it met. It was much easier to fulfil the purposes of the Church in a smaller assembly that took place in the home. Many churches now have home groups as part of their organisational structure, but sometimes they are more social groups rather than serious Bible study groups.

Many, many people have made the link between the home and the early Church and as a result a huge number of house churches have started. It is said that the majority of Christians around the world worship in house churches, but this is probably because of the millions of Christians in China who have been driven underground and who meet in their homes. In the West, Church is changing and many new churches are springing up in coffee bars, workplaces etc, in fact anywhere where there are people gathering. If you are interested in this type of church then read 'Organic Church' by Neil Cole. There are churches that model themselves on the New Testament Church; if you would like to know more about this model you can read 'Rethinking the Wineskin' by Frank Viola, or 'Mega Shift' by James Rutz.

There are many house churches in England that are exactly what the name implies, fully functioning churches in the home. These normally have from 10-30 people and are often linked to house church networks. A similar but different model is 'cell' church, which has a very formal structure with a pastor at the head. The house church has several advantages over the denominational church; firstly, there is no church building to maintain nor are there any paid clergy, so most of their giving can go where it belongs, to the poor. A 1989 survey of churches in America found that 82% of giving went to maintain the building and pay clergy and staff. Secondly, smaller numbers make it easier to fulfil the purposes of the Church, such as loving and encouraging one another, and using one's gifts. Lastly, it is impossible to hide in a house church. How many nominal Christians are there in denominational churches who just turn up on Sunday and that is their church done for the week? Discipleship is vital to encourage Christians and help them to mature, and this can be done more effectively in the house church.

I have briefly mentioned these different models so that you can have an idea of the available alternatives that are out there. However, there are still thousands of churches that are part of denominations which still have buildings and still have clergy and staff, and these are not going away. Some maintain that it would be better to move everyone into house churches and sell the buildings, but that is hardly a practical solution. God has worked and is working in these churches, but it would be good if they were to become more flexible and more in tune with what God is wanting today for His Church and with the needs of their congregations.

A first step would be to make home groups more dynamic. Remember these are only suggestions; it is possible that your home groups are already like this. First of all, I would ask pastors to please only appoint home group leaders who have a pastoring gift. There are so many home group leaders out there who were appointed because they had the correct background or because they appeared dynamic, but they cannot pastor their way out of a paper bag. I can understand how this happens, in that pastors of growing churches are under a lot of pressure to appoint new leaders, but if care is not taken to find people with the correct gifting, it is unfair on the group members and on the leader who will be walking out of God's will. The leader needs good training and accountability. I once prayed for a man who led several groups and he wanted prayer for his addiction to pornography on the internet; nobody knew he was suffering in this way. Where was his accountability? Discipleship is also vital for the group members if they are to walk fully in their calling; they must walk in purity, and discipleship can make sure that they keep on the right path. The group should be a place where members practice their gifts such as teaching, healing and the prophetic as often as possible. A home group should be a place where they focus outside the group as much as inside so that they can use other gifts such as evangelism. One of the most important roles of the leader should be to help each member discover the calling of God on their lives and to help them step out in it.

Worship

At first I thought the answer to the problem of performance worship that was mentioned in the last chapter was for the band to play either at the back or at the side of the church, which is where the organ was positioned in a traditional church and then the focus of the congregation (when they have their eyes open) can be the cross or just the front of the church. However, when you have a truly gifted and spiritually discerning worship leader, being away from the front of church can be a problem. Tim Hughes, who was the worship leader at Soul Survivor, but now leads worship at Holy Trinity Brompton in London, told me that the aim of a worship leader is to usher God's people into His presence and it is very hard to usher in God's people if you cannot see what is happening amongst them. Leading worship has to be a two way interaction, so the leader needs to see the faces of the congregation to discern the mood they are in. The people may appear disheartened, so the leader then has to decide which song to play to help them encounter God in that situation. Tim is very conscious of leading strongly, but at the same time remaining as invisible as possible by not making dramatic movements and by not speaking too much or hyping people up. The key phrase for him is 'gentle authority'.

From what Tim is saying, an anointed worship leader needs to be in the front. Perhaps it would be possible to put the band in one of the front corners of the church and have the leader in a position to see the congregation. This way they would only be peripherally in line of sight and people can then concentrate on the Lord without being distracted by what is happening on the platform.

With regard to getting back to more like it was in New Testament times; allowing the Holy Spirit to have His way and people using their worshipping gifts; Tim Hughes told me that at Soul Survivor they trained people to allow the Holy Spirit to lead them. They taught that you should prepare thoroughly, but then hold it very lightly because the Holy Spirit might be doing something different. He finds it helpful to call someone a 'lead worshipper' rather than a 'worship leader'. Tim described to me a profound time of worship that made a significant impact on him. It was a meeting of 1,000 young people and he was just about to end the worship with a prayer when the leader came up to him and whispered in his ear 'let's just wait; I think God might be doing something'. Tim waited for a bit and then started to sing the refrain 'Praise the Lord, O my soul', which they sang for a few minutes; the band stopped but the congregation continued singing. The leader told them to get off the stage and the singing continued for five or ten minutes. Then someone in the congregation started to sing a song and they all joined in, and after a while people started to sing in the Spirit. Some sang in tongues, some sang their own melodies, some speaking out praise; and this noise built and built and they ended up with cheering, clapping and shouting. Then there was complete silence for a long time until someone else started another song. Tim said *'It was the most perfectly, brilliantly led time of worship I have ever been involved in and I had nothing to do with it. It is one of the few times that I have seen when we were all sensing together where God's Spirit was leading. We worshipped like that with no one on the stage, no one directing it, for 45 minutes. It was one of the most powerful times that I have seen the Spirit move. Lots became Christians that night. It was a profound encounter with God. We got out of the way, everyone owning the time of worship.'*

I was excited to hear this because I did not think it was possible for the worship conditions of the early Church to be re-created in a church of 500-1000 people. Tim agreed that this form of worship needs to happen on a Sunday in church; otherwise our worship will end up just becoming singing and formulaic and something the band provides for everyone else to join in on. It would be so wonderful if this happened in every church on Sunday; this is what worshipping the Lord is all about.

The pastor

The pastor has to be the most difficult job in the world and I would not want to do it for anything. We saw in the last chapter how much work they have to do and it is small wonder that a colossal number of pastors end up burnt out and leave the ministry. In 2001 The Washington Times reported that a third of pastors in the US seriously considered leaving their post in the previous year. A 1991 survey of pastors in the US found that half felt that they were unable to meet the needs of the job. My theory is that pastors burn out because they take on too much responsibility. How can any human being take on the responsibility for the welfare of all their people, plus all the jobs they do in the church and in the community? But as we saw the New Testament Church was not led by a pastor, they had a council of elders that would oversee what was happening, they would have used their gifts, discipled some of the congregation and disciplined others; but their responsibilities would have been shared with other council members and with the Holy Spirit.

It is time for a new wineskin, it is time for the pressure to be taken off the pastor and it is time for the saints to take on the work. I must say at this point how much I love pastors. I know a lot of them and part of my ministry is to help them in any way I can; there is nothing I enjoy more than serving them in some way. I know what a wonderful, sacrificial job most of them do. All pastors do their work to the best of their ability, but too much is asked of them.

What if pastors delegated their tasks to those with gifts and callings in their church? Teachers could preach on Sunday, those with healing gifts could go and visit the sick, intercessors could lead prayers etc. This would mean that the pastor would be free to organise the people, disciple his leaders, sell his vision to the congregation and spend time with the Lord. I am glad to say that there are encouraging signs that some pastors are recognising the fullness of the 'priesthood of all believers'. Within the last month I have heard two visiting pastors, at two different churches, talking about how the pastor should be equipping the saints so that they can serve God effectively in the community. Also two pastors, both of whom are very prophetic, have told me how they are trying to re-structure so that they can be equipping and releasing churches. This is the time for change; it is not easy for a pastor to re-structure his church, but he must do it if he wants to have an effective ministry in the years ahead.

We have been created to use the gifts that God has given us, and if the main work we do is not in our primary gift, then we are in trouble. An example of this is a pastor I know who led his church for years, but he did not have a pastoring gift, so people would eventually get hurt and leave. This church was very strong on worship, healing and the prophetic, but the pastor's lack of pastoring ability negated all his strong giftings. Fortunately he finally realised the situation, left the church and is now majoring in his primary gifting and is being used incredibly powerfully elsewhere in the Body of Christ. So pastors and everyone else, please ensure that you are ministering in your primary gifting. A church clearly needs a good shepherd, so it should be easy enough to appoint one to work alongside the pastor if shepherding is not his gift.

It was mentioned earlier how difficult it is for the Holy Spirit to move in a service when the order of service is rigidly maintained. We also saw how amazingly blessed a service was when the pastor realised that God wanted to do something and told the worship team to get off the stage. The pastor can make a huge difference to a service by being led by the Holy Spirit. It takes a courageous person to do this; it requires them to stand in front of church, with everyone listening, and take the service in a direction that few people are expecting. Rather them than me! Everything in them is saying, 'What happens if I am wrong? What will people think?' But this is what is required every week, so what if the pastor makes a mistake? The more we step out the easier it gets.

If you are a pastor and find that you have difficulty with the Holy Spirit flowing through you; then please go and receive some counselling as I am sure this will help. I talk more about counselling later.

Team Ministry

The Bible advocates team and not hierarchical ministry. I have pointed out the pressures on a pastor and quite frankly I do not believe it is possible for one person to have all the giftings and expertise that are required to fill the role effectively. After all, it is not God's plan that anyone should do it all. Five fold ministry (Ephesians 4:11) is His plan and would solve this problem. It would be the perfect structure in which God's plans can be worked out. I realise that a small church will not have the people available to fill all the roles in the five fold ministry, but in alliances with other churches the resources would be available.

Hierarchical ministry does not work at any level. First of all, it puts the pastor in an impossible position of having to give the impression that he knows everything and can deal with every eventuality, which he obviously can't. No one can. Secondly he has one huge weakness; he is human. We all have weakness that we are born with or that come about through past hurts, and when one person has all the authority in a church, then the hurts in that person affect people all around them. Look at what has happened to the prophetic in the Church. For years the prophetic has been pushed out of the churches in England and it is only now slowly returning. About six years ago I went up to one of the most senior prophets in this nation and asked where the prophets were. She replied 'hiding in caves'. Those with prophetic giftings have had nowhere to go and nobody to understand them, because pastors have not received them due to the mess they cause. What I mean by that is that prophetic people are difficult to pastor because they often feel that they have heard from God and do not understand why the pastor does not jump when they speak. A prophetic word can be given at the wrong time, in the wrong way or even when it is meant for prayer and not to be spoken at all, and any of these can cause a dreadful problem for the poor pastor. Those pastors, for instance, who have suffered rejection in the past will find prophets particularly hard to deal with as they will feel out of control. So it is understandable that the pastor would rather keep the prophetic out of his church if he cannot cope with sorting out the problems that come with it; after all he is human and he has enough to do anyway. It is understandable but it is not biblical. The Bible makes it very clear how important the prophetic is.

'Follow the way of love and eagerly desire spiritual gifts, especially the gift of prophecy.' (1 Corinthians 14:1)

Pastors need to have the prophets discipled, taught and released, not suppressed. All these problems disappear if the church is run by a five fold ministry and not just one pastor. In this situation there would be a prophetic figure on the team who can give an understanding of how a prophet thinks; he can teach prophecy in the church and help people to mature in the gifting. The pastor on the team can disciple them and any messes can be cleared up between them. Everyone wins.

The same thing happened with intercession. The gift of intercession is a prophetic one and again many pastors felt that they could not cope with these individuals who made life difficult for them. Often the intercessor is able to hear from God more clearly than the pastor and it will not take much of an unhealed hurt in the pastor to make this a very intimidating situation. Intercessors are vital for the Church and for the pastor as they can identify problems coming up in the church, and their prayers can be a wall of protection around the pastor and his family, Yet I know many intercessors who have either left their church and set up their own ministry or are sitting in their churches ignored by their pastor. I have a good friend in America who is prophetic and an intercessor and she is a humble woman of God. Several years ago she started an intercession group that quickly grew to 60 people and they sought the Lord on what His plans were for their church and how they should pray. She also did a lot of teaching on intercession. She was in a large, well known church. One day some of the leadership came to visit her and her husband, and told them that the leadership already knew which direction to take the church, so they did not need any intercessors, and she was told to close the group down.

Again, the weaknesses in the pastor that prevent him from relating to the intercessor can be negated through team ministry. We all have weaknesses and issues in our lives from past hurts; the effect of these on the church can be hugely lessened when a team deals with a problem, because one man's weakness is another man's strength.

I associate mainly with people who are on fire for the Lord, hungry to learn as much as possible and wanting to be used by the Lord, but many of these are only loosely connected to a church because there are so few churches that understand them. I have also been on a few mission trips with teams from America and several of the people on the team have told me that their pastors did not know they were on the trip and they didn't care. Now these are not loose cannons; these are godly, hungry, gifted men and women who want to grow and move on in their calling, but they can find no support or understanding from their pastors. It is not all doom and gloom; I have met people on these trips who say that they were prayed for by the pastor before they left, or they are being prayed for by the church while they are away, or that they will be able to tell the church about what happened on the mission when they return. That is fantastic for those people, but this should happen in all churches and team ministry can help in this.

Hierarchical leadership, as in the Anglican Church, not only inflicts the weaknesses of the leader on the congregation, but it also allows the work of a good pastor to be cancelled by a successor with different beliefs. This is not a new problem. William Haslam in his wonderful autobiography 'From Death unto Life', written in the 1860's, quotes one of his parishioners who is upset at the thought of Haslam leaving the parish after bringing the church and the area into revival:

'This teaching seems all true and scriptural; but what will become of us if you go away and another man comes and thinks otherwise? We have no security that conversion work will go on and living souls be fed and encouraged. Very few churches have such a work as the Lord is doing here!'

Team ministry would bring stability as one person leaving would not be so disruptive.

Equipping the saints

The reason why so many hungry people go outside the church for food is because they do not receive it inside. They are looking for a place that pervades the atmosphere of the Holy Spirit, a place where they can be equipped and a place where they can be used. Equipping the saints can answer two of these needs. Unquestionably the most important area of equipping is in teaching people how to hear God; it is impossible for anyone to step out in their calling if they cannot hear God. There are many ways to hear God and we need to be taught them, and we need to be taught how to hear Him better day by day. We need to be taught about anything that would help us serve God in a better and more powerful way. There need to be courses on pastoring, preaching, healing, the prophetic, intercession, spiritual warfare, evangelising etc, in fact anything that is mentioned in the Bible. In addition there should be teaching on subjects like the poor and politics. There is a Christian University near Washington DC in America that majors on training students on how to succeed in the political arena. If we are to change society we need more Christians in politics.

Now I can just hear the pastors shouting out that they do not have the people, the time or the resources to teach all this, but this again is where the five-fold ministries come in. It says in Ephesians 4:11-12:

'It was he who gave some to be apostles, some to be prophets, some to be evangelists, and some to be pastors and teachers, to prepare God's people for works of service, so that the body of Christ may be built up.'

These are the people who do the equipping. Many of the people I meet at conferences and on missions would be ideal teachers of many of these subjects; many churches have people like this to draw on. If you do not have the resources in your church then find people within the networks that you are connected with or send your people to a church that does, or send them to one of the travelling ministries. Sharon Stone goes around the UK teaching how to hear God and on other giftings such as intercession. At the time of writing she is teaching a large church that had never been exposed to this before, so that intercessors, watchmen and prophets can be raised up in the church. She is doing a vital job in the Body of Christ as the Church in this country cannot move forward without these giftings being activated.

I am genuinely puzzled as to why most churches do not teach these subjects; it may be pastors' not being keen to expose their flock to someone else's teaching, but it is probably just that they are in the wrong mindset.

All teaching, including the sermon, would be more effective if questions were allowed during the meeting to clarify points, as they were in the early church. It is hard doing this in a church meeting with 300 people but it would be fine in smaller meetings. People grow much more when they are participating as opposed to just sitting and listening all the time.

Counselling

Thankfully counselling is gaining more credibility in the Body of Christ. We all come to Christ with baggage from our life up to that point: hurts from past boyfriends or girlfriends, rejection, bad relationships with a parent or sibling; whatever it is these things create hurts that affect our relationship with Christ and with other people, and make us far less effective Christians. We develop strongholds in our minds, lies about ourselves and about Christ, and these strongholds need to be pulled down. Even at birth we inherit generational problems that come down through the family line; anger can be one of these or some sort of sickness.

I have already mentioned how these hurts can affect a pastor; the same applies to each and every one of us. For us to fulfil our callings effectively we need to be whole human beings and we need help to free us from what binds us, although occasionally the Holy Spirit comes in and heals us without the need for outside assistance.

Ten years ago there were very few people who you could go to for help, but more recently several ministries have been raised up. One of my godchildren had a breakdown a few years ago due to the war that was going on between her parents who had divorced. Fortunately the problem was recognised by one of her teachers and it was clear that she needed counselling, but I could not find any Christian counsellor in London who specialised in children. Thankfully that is not the case now. The pioneers in this ministry were John and Paula Sandford of Elijah House (www.elijahhouse.org) and they were followed by others, including a ministry out of Bill Hamon's church, Christian International, called Restoring the Foundations (www.healinghouse.org). Both these ministries train up people all around the world. I know senior pastors who go every year to have counselling to make sure that they have not developed any wrong mindsets and so that they can flow freely in their calling. I recommend that every pastor goes through counselling at least once for their own sakes and for the sake of their congregation. This is something very simple but it will probably have life changing consequences.

I will give an example from my own life. I am not a very dramatic example because I was fortunate in that I have had quite an easy and privileged life and upbringing, but I still had issues to deal with. Around five years ago a good friend looked at me intently and asked me if I had ever had counselling, and on hearing that I hadn't she told me to go to Elijah House. Now this woman is very prophetic and I knew this came from the Lord, so I promptly went to Elijah House for four days. During my time there we dealt with issues that came up as a result of my having been at boarding school and a few other things. To be honest, I did not notice any change in myself; but a few weeks later when I went to help my friend while she ministered in Russia, the first thing she said to me, even before saying 'hello', was that I had changed.

One of the regrets in my Christian walk was that I had never felt the love of God and hardly ever felt the power of the Holy Spirit in me. Now I know that feelings are not vital, but I am afraid they were to me and I was especially desperate to feel the love of God. Last year I thought it was time to have some more counselling to try and remove anything that was holding me back from receiving from the Holy Spirit. Sharon Stone told me about Restoring the Foundations, part of Bill Hamon's network and she knew a wonderful woman who ministered in Atlanta with her husband. So off I went for five three hour sessions in two and a half days. They went through every part of my life and, having identified a number of strongholds, they proceeded to pray them off me; after I had repented, forgiven etc. Most of my wrong thinking was about me, how I did not think I was worthy of God's love, how I had no confidence in myself etc. I came back with a list of new truths for my life that I spoke out every day for a few months so that I would come to get rid of the old lies and get in the habit of accepting the new truths. A few months later I had the breakthrough I had been waiting for so long, while I was ministering in Ukraine. I had no expectations of what was going to happen. God just came in and did it and ever since I have been moving forward in an exciting new way.

Some people think that we should just 'tough it out' when we have these problems and not to over-spiritualise them, but that is not God's way. These problems are of a spiritual nature and God has provided wonderful people who are skilled in this ministry, so we should use them. We must be careful not to exhibit individualist tendencies; we must be humble and seek help from the Body. So pastors, please train up people who can act as counsellors in your church; it is so important and every church needs someone doing this ministry. We need a church without stain or wrinkle as it says in Ephesians 5:27.

'and to present her to himself as a radiant church, without stain or wrinkle or any other blemish, but holy and blameless.'

I believe that each person should be ministering effectively, but this cannot really happen unless they are free of the demonic influences in their lives. I know of three large churches in Ukraine that believe that being 'saved' (Greek word, sozo) includes healing and deliverance as well as salvation, so each new believer goes through healing and deliverance ministry. There are many churches around the world that practice this and consequently they have new believers who are freed from anything that might hold them back and who are ready to minister powerfully in the name of Jesus. I am sure there are some churches that practice this in the UK but the vast majority of churches do not. I urge you pastors to look into this type of ministry and introduce it into your churches.

Callings

There is little point in equipping people for works of service if they have no idea what their calling is. A few years ago I used to ask people what their giftings were, then I started to ask what their calling was and I was shocked by the response. First of all, most had never been asked these questions before, some did not even know what I meant by 'calling', and then on thinking about it many had no idea what to say. I would say that maybe 10% came up with an answer. Again I know that this is not a comprehensive poll, but my experience tells me that this is a common situation.

It is vital that the importance of knowing what God has called you to do is regularly taught in churches. At the same time room has to be made to accommodate people who want to be used. One church that I was closely associated with decided to introduce a course that helped identify giftings. Part of the course requires people to fill in a questionnaire with around 100 questions on different things one does in ministry. There might be a question like 'do you like praying for the sick?' and you had to indicate 0-5 on how much you liked doing this. Having completed the questionnaire you put your marks on a grid, each column representing a gifting and when you added up your score you could see what your predominate giftings were. I have done this three times and each time there was a change in my score, because over time our giftings change in emphasis and intensity. For me the one common denominator was that I always scored close to zero for 'evangelism'. After much of the church had gone through this exercise, they were all fired up and ready to use their gifts, but there were only a few opportunities to use them in the church, and so there were a lot of frustrated people.

In my travels I have looked for churches that equip and release people in their callings, so far I have only found a few. I went to visit a church in Cornwall that I had heard about, but I was surprised that there were only about 25 people there. The pastor obviously knew what I was thinking because he told me that the reason there were so few people in the church was because the rest were ministering elsewhere. The pastor said that he would be happy if there was nobody there on Sundays as it would mean that the congregation were using their giftings and fulfilling their callings. The pastor of a church I know well in London takes a similar view; he would be thrilled if he had an empty church!

Another example is an exceptional church that I would like to tell you about in some detail, here and a little later on. Any church would be greatly blessed if they took on some of the ideas mentioned below. The church is called 'The Embassy of the Blessed Kingdom of God for All Nations', it is based in Kiev, Ukraine and is the largest church in Europe. The church is pastored by Pastor Sunday Adelaja, who is a Nigerian and a wonderful man of God.

God does work in mysterious ways, as He called a black man from Nigeria
to start a church in a country where there were virtually no black people. As
a new believer Pastor Sunday was looking to go to University somewhere,
but he needed a scholarship, and with the Lord's leading he chose to go to
Byelarussian State University in the former Soviet Union. After two weeks he
wanted to go home but the Lord told him to stay. He joined an underground
church and proceeded with his studies until the Lord told him to move to Kiev.
In 1993 he began his church with seven members. Now some 12,000 meet in
an old indoor athletics centre, and there are another some 12,000 that meet in
the 34 daughter churches in Kiev, in addition there are another 275 churches
that are part of his network in 30 countries. Furthermore, his church was very
influential in the Orange Revolution that overthrew the communist government
a few years ago. He is now close to forty years old and the Lord has blessed me
by connecting me with him from time to time. Two years ago I was invited by
a pastor friend to have lunch with Pastor Sunday and, during a conversation, I
told him of my sadness that so few churches helped saints walk in their calling.
He suggested that I came to his church for five days to see what they do.

I went to Kiev in August 2005 and I was allowed to see anything I wanted.
When someone comes to the Lord in the church service they are taken by
a pastor to another room where they will make a proper repentance. They
then spend three evenings doing 'Meeting with Jesus' where they are healed,
delivered and filled with the Spirit. Unless they need special help, like for
addiction, they go immediately into a home group and at the same time they
will go through a 12 week course (a type of Alpha course). The pastor will
report to a senior pastor on how many passed the course, stayed in church etc.
If they pass through to this point they will then do a seven week course that
may last 26 weeks, depending on progress, called 'Discovery of the person's
potential'. So right at the beginning they start to help people find out their
giftings and calling. From then on this is reinforced all the way across the
church beginning with Pastor Sunday.

After a couple of services on the Sunday I was there, I interviewed around 20 people to find out if people really did know what their calling was and if the church was helping them to step out in it. Here is a sample of the notes I took at the time. RUSSELAND was homeless; the church paid for an operation on his eyes; they paid for a flat while he was at Bible School. He received healing when he came to the Lord and he is going to have a ministry to the homeless. SERGEI has been in the church two years. He was healed of a heart condition when he came to the Lord. He helps new Christians. VLADAMIR, a young Russian who came to the Lord two years earlier, spent one year in rehab and one year at the Bible School. He was healed instantly of alcohol, cigarettes and drug addiction. As soon as I asked him what he was going to be he said 'pastor'. He is going back to minister in Russia. SERGEI, a young man who was an alcoholic and a drug addict, was taken out of a ditch and the Lord healed him. He does not know what his calling is yet, but it is something he is thinking about and wants to move into. VLADAMIR has been a believer for seven months and although he does not know his calling yet the church is talking to him about it. I wrote about these people two years ago and tears come my eyes as I am reminded of the beautiful things that God is doing in that church.

Pastor Sunday says that every person is born for a purpose on this earth and he really does try to ensure that the people in his church fulfil that purpose. Every person I spoke to either knew what their calling was or they were working on finding out, when I asked them if the church was helping them discover their calling, the answer was always 'yes'. Releasing every person into their calling really is in the DNA of the church; it permeates everywhere. I shall be writing in the next chapter in more detail about three remarkable women I met at that church.

I spoke to pastor Vitali, who is one of only seven full time paid pastors. He is studying at University, has a wife and three children, he has a group of 30 leaders and under them another 700 and finally he works between 4am and 6am on building his house that will be finished in two years. He told me 'My understanding of life is that I have to help every person I meet in my life. When a person comes to my home group I am not interested in how he can be useful for the church, I am interested in how can I help him or her to release his or her potential.' What a remarkable statement. We need to have this sort of thinking in all our churches. He encouraged and helped a woman in his group start a business and she earned $1.2m in 2004.

The church is radical in many ways. I am relating this as it may give you some ideas for your church. They have all night prayer (11pm-7am) EVERY weekday in the main church and many others in daughter churches. The whole church fasts for 11 days every summer and 2,000 go to a camp for a water fast. Pastor Sunday told one of his pastors to have services in the main street of Kiev at the weekend as it is closed to traffic at that time. In June 2005 they started services in the street, on Saturday 3pm-5pm for children and then 5pm-9pm for adults, on Sunday 3pm-9pm. Around 300 give their life to the Lord each service. There are a lot of drugs and alcohol abuse in the country and each church has a rehab and a soup kitchen where they serve 800 to 2000 meals a day, and many come to the Lord.

Pastor Sunday encourages his people to get involved with all aspects of society, including politics. As mentioned, this is something we need to do in the United Kingdom. Currently the Mayor of Kiev is a Christian and a member of pastor Sunday's church and when there was a plan for a Gay March through the city the Mayor vetoed it. Just think what could be done if the Mayor of London was a Christian.

What I have described in this section is the core message of this book. We must help envision the people, help them to discover their potential and help them to achieve their goals. In the next chapter I give examples of what can happen if we do this.

Love

Clearly love is the most important ingredient of a church, but I do not know many churches that flow in it. I was at one late last year in Nikolaev, Ukraine. It does not really matter where it was, I might just as easily have been in England or the US. I was on a trip that was led by my friend Holly Miller under the ministry of Randy Clark and my role was head of intercession, which took place during the worship and preaching at each service. There was a team of about 15 local intercessors. All but two were women and they were led by a remarkable young woman called Natasha. We were with them for three days. Services took place in a building with a large stage that had a curtain across it, behind which the intercession took place.

During my time there I observed this group of intercessors and I discerned that there was a significant amount of love between them. Before each service they hugged one another for maybe five minutes at a time, and spent time ministering to one another. On the final morning, as I came onto the stage behind the curtain, I noticed again small groups of intercessors just loving one another. As I came into the middle of the stage one of them noticed me and came running over to give me a big hug, and then another came to hug me and then another. Around eight of them came to show me their love; there were no words because we did not speak each other's language and I did not have an interpreter with me. At the final service I gathered the group together to tell them how wonderful they were and when I finished several came closer and one by one they touched my arm and said 'I love you' or something similar. They then asked if they could pray for me and for the next twenty minutes they all prayed for me.

I am telling you this because during my time there the Lord broke through to me, showing me His love, and as a result my sensitivity to the Holy Spirit increased substantially. This breakthrough came partly through the ministry of love from Natasha who prayed for me during my visit and partly from the atmosphere of love that I found amongst those intercessors. When the Lord is amongst us and love is abroad, strongholds come down and breakthroughs occur. I spoke to the pastor of the church who told me that this love flowed down through the whole church and he believed that it came out of his emphasis on relationships.

One of my friends understands the importance of love in his church. Michael is the assistant pastor of a church in the US that was hit by a move of God a few years ago and has been experiencing the renewing power of the Holy Spirit ever since. I spoke to him the other day and asked if signs and wonders were still taking place in the church, he replied that he did not care; all he wanted was for the love of God to flow through the church.

This is so important and we need to focus on this in all our churches, as individualism and the breakdown of the family unit are infecting the Church and society. It has been reported that Muslims who convert to Christianity in the UK find it difficult because they come out of a very strong family environment into the church which they find falls well short of their expectations, which have been built by reading about the love of Jesus in the Bible.

But what can we do in our churches to increase the love there? Well, of course, the main ingredient is the Lord's presence, but I do not profess to have an answer as to how to guarantee that. An indication of something that might help is in the example above, where the pastor says that he puts an emphasis on relationships. If the pastor and his/her wife/husband are full of the love of the Lord then that love will flow down through the church. A practical suggestion that might help is the restoration of the love feast of the New Testament Church. In studying revivals in Cornwall I found that several revivals began during the quarterly Methodist love feast. There is something about people coming together to testify to what God has done in their lives and to share a meal. A church near me offers food to everyone after the service, which encourages people to fellowship together.

Because I had not seen any example of a church flowing in the love of Jesus apart from my experience in Ukraine, I wrote an e-mail to many of my contacts to ask if anyone had come across such a church. I explained that experiencing love from people putting on conferences did not count; the love had to flow as a normal part of every day church activity. I received very few positive replies, but three people mentioned a church in Tacoma, Washington, called Destiny

City Church. I had heard quite a bit about the ministry of this church, as some churches I knew had taken on some of their teaching, but I had no direct experience, so I recently went to a one day conference to hear about the church for myself.

The conference speaker was Mike Riches, who was the senior pastor for 24 years until he and his wife left to head up the church's International ministry, and he has an extraordinary story to tell. He came from a legalistic Baptist background and he was having some success with his church that had grown from 170 to 1700 in seven years. The church was strong on verse-by-verse expositional preaching, they had a noted children's ministry and a vibrant young adult church. They seemed to be doing the right things; they were trying to equip the saints and the church was growing. However, whilst on holiday in 2000, Mike read 1 Corinthians 4:19-20:

'But I will come to you very soon, if the Lord is willing, and then I will find out not only how these arrogant people are talking, but what power they have. For the kingdom of God is not a matter of talk but of power.'

The word that really impacted him was 'power' and he contemplated this throughout his holiday. Within the next four months the church experienced things they had never seen before: several people had dramatic demonic manifestations, many physical healings took place, prophetic words and dreams were released and his wife experienced two angelic visitations to explain what was going on. This invasion of the Holy Spirit continued, and three years later 70% of those attending the church had left, largely because God had offended their minds (again tradition getting on the way of a new move of God). Many came to replace those who left.

This move of God continues today and now Mike and his wife are travelling around, telling their story and showing how what they have learned can be introduced into any church. A large part of their teaching is around what they call 'freedom prayer' that involves training people to hear God and then releasing them to pray in twos or threes for people to be released from generational curses, emotional hurts and demonic strongholds.

Mike Riches spoke about love being a servant of our will. We are commanded to love and they teach the truth about what love is. They teach strongly on humility and servant hood and they hold their people accountable. They often ask their people to go through 1 Corinthians 13 4-8 inserting their names instead of the word 'love'; for instance Michael is kind, Michael does not envy etc. They are keen to equip and say that 80% of equipping is equipping the heart. They teach people to be more like Jesus so that they can be Jesus to others. I love this and it would be wonderful if churches would teach like this, as from all accounts it works; it creates an environment of love in the church.

God is doing a new thing and we need a new wineskin to enable His plans to be properly fulfilled. I have listed above some suggestions as to how the Church could change to allow the saints to be envisioned, equipped and sent out to fulfil their callings. In the final chapter I give some suggestions as to how we can step out in our calling.

CHAPTER 9

What we can do to step out in our calling

God has some special things for you to do, things which He has prepared in advance for you to do. Ephesians 2:10 says:

'For we are God's workmanship, created in Christ Jesus to do good works, which God prepared in advance for us to do.'

Do you want to do these things or are you content to sit in church each Sunday and just sing a few songs, listen to a sermon and leave? You were made by God to do the things He has called you to do. He wants you to fulfil your destiny, not out of duty or a desire for favour but because you love Him. Paul says in Philippians 2:15 that we are to *'shine like stars in the universe';* do you want to shine like a star or are you content where you are? When the Lord asks you to do something for Him, you can say no; He has given you the choice. Cindy Jacobs, a wonderful prophet to the nations, had a visitation from an angel (he may have been the Lord) who asked her if she wanted the ministry he was offering. Now Cindy knew that there would be a great cost if she accepted, and as she was considering her response the angel said that she was not the first person who had been asked, but the others had turned him down.

Each of us has received a divine inheritance from Christ which is our responsibility to fulfil.

'I pray also that the eyes of your heart may be enlightened in order that you may know the hope to which he has called you, the riches of his glorious inheritance in the saints,' (Ephesians 1:18)

Each of us will be held responsible and we will have to give an account of how we handled our inheritance. In the parable of the talents the one who received

159

only one talent hid it in the ground for fear of risking it and he was accused of being a 'wicked and lazy servant.' Many people are happy to just go to church and be anonymous, but that is just not an option as a Christian. Bill Hamon in his book 'The Day of the Saints' says:

'The full meaning of saint is one who is 100 percent sold out to God, on fire for Christ, holy and set apart for the Master's use. Even the term "lukewarm" saint is a contradiction of terms. A true saint is not lukewarm. Even saying that there will be Christians who will not participate is a contradiction, for the word "Christ" in Greek means 'the anointed one'".

For me some of the most terrifying words in the Bible are:

'I know your deeds, that you are neither cold nor hot. I wish you were either one or the other! So, because you are lukewarm-- neither hot nor cold-- I am about to spit you out of my mouth.' (Revelation 3:15-16)

I just cannot conceive how I would feel if the Lord said that to me. It is just not an option for us to be cold or lukewarm; we must do everything we can to fulfil what He has called us to, whatever the perceived cost to us, our families or our work. God knows our situation and He would never call us to something we cannot do.

This nation is in a terrible condition and with the undermining of our Judeo Christian values the situation is going to get worse. The nation needs Christians to rise up and take their place in society.

Many people have the wrong mindset; they do not realise what they can achieve. If you just stay all the time in one church, and you do not read about what the Lord is doing around the world, you will have a very narrow viewpoint and your vision will be restricted. If you are someone who understands the unlimited power of God, you can achieve things in partnership with God that you cannot even imagine.

Some of you may know about the artist Akiane (www.artakiane.com) who at four had a life-changing spiritual transformation that resulted in bringing the family to God. At that time she started to paint, and at seven she started writing poetry that sometimes comes to her in a complete form. The inspiration for her art and literature comes from her visions, dreams, observations of people, nature and God. Her paintings are so wonderful that people who own them say that there is an atmosphere that comes out of the painting, that the painting has life that you can step into it. This sounds incredible but why should it? Cannot God create anything, either through us or on His own? Akiane co-operates with God and He uses her to create these wonderful things. Now God can do this with any of us; He can use us to invent the cure for cancer, new technologies or new fuels and I believe that indeed Christians will come up with these inventions; if they haven't already. Ephesians 3:20 says:

'Now to him who is able to do immeasurably more than all we ask or imagine, according to his power that is at work within us.'

Expand your mind. God is doing unimaginable signs and wonders around the world, things that the world has never seen before (at least there are no reports on record) such as gold fillings in teeth, gold dust and gem stones. People question these, saying why should God do these things? But why shouldn't He and who are we to question what God does? Everything needs to be tested to make sure it is from God, so get the views of people who you respect, who have seen these things. The point is, don't have a closed mind, believe in the impossible. Believe that whatever you do at the leading of the Lord, He has part in it. If you are doing what you are called to do, the Lord can use you to influence people and make a difference in the nation. It may take 20 years, as it did with William Wilberforce to abolish the slave trade, or you could make a difference in a moment. God wants you to be passionate for Him and passionate to serve Him. Romans 12:11 says:

'Never be lacking in zeal, but keep your spiritual fervour, serving the Lord.'

Wherever you are, in the workplace, with your friends and family or in church; look for opportunities to use the gifts God has given you, be proactive not reactive. If you have compassion for the sick and you see someone sick in your office, ask if you could pray for them. If you know someone is going through a difficult time, get alongside them and maybe tell them you are praying for them. Take every opportunity to show the people around you the love of Jesus. Ask the Lord every day for opportunities to be used by Him. I would be surprised if you could not find at least one situation every day where you could be used by God.

To show you what one can achieve through co-operating with God I am going to relate the stories of three remarkable women I interviewed while at pastor Sunday's church in Kiev, Ukraine. I am sure there are similar women all over the world, but I just happened to find these in Ukraine. These women started off no different from any of us and yet they partnered with God and achieved more than they could have hoped for.

a)　Natalya

As a young woman Natalya had some disease that meant she could not have children. God told her to go to the church of Pastor Sunday. At the first meeting Pastor Sunday had a word of knowledge about her disease and said that in nine months time she would give birth. She did. Natalya said 'Pastor always teaches that the period before repentance is the period of preparation, and when you are with God you can use everything you have gone through.' 'I understood that my calling was big, I knew this was my land but what I was going to do with it, I didn't know. I got a book of Pastor's called; "Fulfil your Calling" and everything began from that book. I was reading that book and in the middle of it I saw a vision. There was a big seven story building.' She went and told Pastor Sunday and he told her to write down the vision and wait. She wrote it down and forgot about it. Two years later she was in a conference and God said, 'I want you to seek your calling' and Pastor Sunday came up to her and took her by the lapels and said, 'you sow your school, you sow your school; and she said 'what school?' That was on the 29th August and on the 2nd October she opened her arts and music school and now has more than 3,000 students with daughter structures in other places. Many come to the Lord through these schools.

b)   Pastor Victoria

Pastor Victoria at 29 was very successful, being highly regarded by politicians and socially moving in high circles. She came to the Lord four years before my visit; she always knew that her calling was outside the church rather than in it. Victoria waited until, in her words, she, 'received revelation into my spirit and my heart about my land'. The Russian word for area of calling is 'land'. Her vision was to have centres to, 'enlighten everyone's heart and to release them from the burden that they have, the mentality they have. People can come to the centre from the church or from the world because the centre is directed to the world.' Her aim was to change the Eastern European Communist mentality of being a follower and from being controlled. 'My goal is to make them doers, to restore a person with God's love. First of all people come to get this attention and care and we teach people to dream.' She gets nothing from the government as they are very suspicious of such organisations. 'Our pastor teaches us to believe in the impossible' (I heard that a lot). Twelve people came the first time, in a month there were 40, in another month 70, in two more months there were 500. To date 1,500 have been through the nine month course where there are 22 subjects that can be learned. The aim is to re-educate people and change their mindsets. Two girls came from a Striptease club, but she did not tell them that they had to give up their jobs. They began praying in the territory of their call. They evangelised their customers and eventually the club closed. She wants to train up a team. 'Ten people will turn Ukraine upside down'. Most of the people come from outside the church and when I asked how many became Christians, she said 'nearly all of them'. 'Most people stay in their jobs but they influence their surroundings.'

c)   Tatyana Galushko

Tatyana says she is not a pastor; I think she is mistaken. She has written a book about her early life called 'When You Can't Live and Yet You Can't Die'. She had a terrible childhood and then ran away pretty young to become a drug addict and prostitute for about ten years. She led a life of degradation, her husband was murdered and later she tried to commit suicide, but in 1999 when she was 25, she gave her life to the Lord. She went back to finish school and did very well and then went to Bible School. Later she had a vision that she must try to help school teenagers to make sure that they did not end up like her. She was asked to speak at a school a few times and then they asked for a written program, so she went away and wrote it in seven months.

In 2002 she wrote down her vision and Pastor Sunday told her that only those who have been proven faithful in small things can be given more, so he suggested that she start with small steps. She was quite offended by him. After two weeks she was praying and she saw herself as a small seed falling into the ground. 'God gave me a vision about the School Ministry. My God gave me a fire in my heart; I want to raise future generations who know the Kingdom of God.' In the course of three months she was unsuccessful so she went back to Pastor Sunday and asked him what he was trying to teach her. 'He helped in the first steps and as a father he was there to see how I was doing and he was interested in me.' God opened doors and she found favour with State organisations. Tatyana has entry to 120 schools in and around Kiev. In May 2005 there was a new law passed that allows the teaching of Christian values in schools so they are expecting the program to explode. In the month after my visit there was a Council of Social Services meeting and Tatyana was to present her program at the meeting. She was expecting to get into schools all over the country. The children targeted are aged 14-17. She and her team go into schools to teach and then the children can go to clubs after school where there will be more Christian input and from there they will be guided into church. She also gets the children into summer camps. She meets with parents and teachers as well. She was about to start a ministry for prostitutes at the time of my visit.

I asked her what her vision was for the next five years. She got out a piece of paper and started writing furiously, laying out her vision. By the time she is 70 she hopes to have reached one billion people through her book and program. She has had breakthrough in Kiev and the surrounding district, so she has delegated to others those two areas and she is focusing on the whole of Ukraine. 'Every person that has come to know Jesus as his Saviour in the Lord has to be the head and not the tail'. 'Everything that you pass through in your life is your source that you can use for the benefit of other people.'

At this point I would like to tell you something about myself. I am just an ordinary person and God has used me in different ways, so my story may help you to step out in your calling. The church I am in is a good church in many ways, but I have never been asked what my passion is, what my calling is, or encouraged in any way to fulfil my destiny. This may be because my interests are in the prophetic and spiritual warfare and most churches find such subjects tricky, or it may be because they just do not understand the importance of Ephesians 4:12. Whatever the reason, I have hardly ever been used in the church and anything that I have achieved has been because of the Lord's mercy and any giftings that He has put in me.

I came to the Lord in 1987 and until 1994 I just helped do anything that was needed in the church: welcoming, stewarding, serving etc. I was 37 when I became a Christian and I was an accountant and a businessman who was bursting with ideas to help my church but these were all ignored. I definitely wanted to be noticed by the pastor and was looking for affirmation in my insecurity, but some of my ideas were good ones. I am sure that I came under the 'difficult' category, but I wish someone had come to me and told me of my weaknesses and helped me to be healed. Eventually I was healed, through my own initiative, but it was years later.

My life changed in 1994 when God told me to go to Toronto and I experienced the Holy Spirit for the first time. Since 1987 I had been keen to serve God in any way that I could, but after Toronto I wanted to find out more about the supernatural side of God. I was involved with the outpouring in England in 1994, visiting different churches and seeing the Holy Spirit touch them for the first time. After this I began to research where to go and find out more about the supernatural. I went to any healing or prophetic conference I could and made sure that every speaker prayed for me as many times as possible. I wanted the anointing to do the things they were doing and I went to many conferences in America as they were far more advanced in the supernatural.

One of the first conferences I went to was in St Louis where I heard about spiritual warfare for the first time. This subject really interested me, so I started to read the books of Cindy Jacobs and others and I have been involved in this, in some way or another, ever since.

An important trip was when I went to Brazil on a team of 100 with Randy Clark where I prayed for many sick people. As many of you will know, if you are not a pastor, the number of people that you can minister to is very limited, so it was great to pray for people for hours at a time. I cannot say that masses of people were healed, but some were and it was very encouraging. If you want to step out I would strongly recommend that you go abroad on a team like I did. I am not sure why, but the Lord gives one something extra as you go and minister in a foreign country.

About ten years ago I began a new aspect of my ministry. A minister I knew was putting on a conference in London and she knew that I had a comfortable car (old, but comfortable) so she asked me if I would drive some of the speakers around. Knowing her, the Lord directed her to ask me. These were all well known American prophets, intercessors and healing ministers. I jumped at the opportunity because I hoped that some of their anointing would rub off on me, and to be honest there was still a little of the 'wanting to be noticed' in me at that time. Because we were the same sort of age I became friends with some of them. When I was in my twenties I had wanted to be someone who networked business people, but I was lousy at it as I always misjudged them. Through going to many conferences and through driving the speakers around, I met many pastors, and before I knew it I was beginning to network people and doing what I had always wanted to do. When networking for Kingdom purposes

I find that God gives me favour and He has brought forth some rather special things through this work.

Something else that I was interested in from pre-Christian times was history. I was an avid reader of history when I was at school, although they were only novels, and the only 'A' level I passed was History. After school I graduated to reading pure history books, but I gave these up around 1990 when I discovered books on the great saints of the past like John Wesley, George Whitfield etc. I was so excited to read about what these great men and women achieved through faith in Jesus Christ. Now my love of history developed into a love of the land and the Lord told me to go and pray over the nation, so this is what I do from time to time. As part of that I have recently started a website www. christianheritage.org on which I am going to put short biographies of around 75 great saints and photos of places where they were born, died, had revivals etc. I am hoping that when completed it will go into churches so that people will learn about our great Christian heritage that has been ignored by many for too long. I never cease to wonder at God's goodness in allowing me to use my passion for history for Kingdom purposes.

My passion for the supernatural continued and my hunger for more took me to the revival in Pensacola, Florida four times and an intercessors conference in Colorado seven times. I was growing, but my accountant's mind kept getting in the way, however my hunger enabled me to press on despite that. I was very excited when a young man called Todd Bentley came onto the scene a few years ago. This hunger for more has led me into another side of my ministry, encouraging as many people as possible to experience the Glory realm, so I have a list of quite a few people whom I keep informed of conferences in England. I encourage as many as possible to get involved with these extraordinarily gifted people like Todd Bentley. I wanted to do the things Todd was doing, namely being used to heal many and having close encounters with God, so I went on his team to Uganda. This was the first of several trips to Africa and the Lord has used me increasingly to heal people. In my networking capacity the Lord has used a gift He has placed in me of being culturally empathetic. God has enabled me to build friendships with different cultural groups, and to make friends with pastors I met in Africa. They have since invited me back to preach in different churches and to pray for the sick. This is new for me because I had never preached in a church before, but I believe that this is something that is going to happen increasingly in the future.

I have tried to show how I have pushed forward and the Lord has opened the doors. Sometimes I have felt that I have just fallen into things by accident, but later I see that God's hand has been on them. I have been encouraged along the way by many prophetic words over my life; a side benefit of knowing so many prophetic people. Most of these words have been encouraging and confirming rather than directional and I suppose the Lord gave me these words as He realised that I was not very good at hearing His voice and needed some help. Over the years I have been able to hear His voice more clearly, which is a great blessing. The only side of my ministry that I have not mentioned is my writing; I have not a clue where this came from. I have never been keen on any sort of writing, but one day in a car a very prophetic man turned around in his seat and gave me one of my few directional words. He said, 'You must write a book called, "God's Heart for a Dying Land"', so I did. Stepping out sometimes happens this way.

As you read this you may be thinking that you do not have the time to do any more than you do as family, work etc fill up all your time. If you are thinking this way please consider the following story. Billy Bray was born in Cornwall in 1794 and was a tin miner and preacher. Billy was renowned for his great joy in his Saviour and he would often dance and shout praises to the Lord. He had a wife and seven children and worked full time in the tin mine, and yet he still had time to lead many people to the Lord and to build three chapels. In 1838 he discerned the Lord telling him that he must build a chapel a little distant from his home. A man gave him the land and after digging the foundations he went to find some stone to build with. Billy had no money whatever to pay for this venture, so he had to rely on the Lord for the provision of everything. He put it on Billy's heart to go to a place where some people had already dug out some stone and it looked as though there was none left, but he started to dig and found all he needed. He would finish at the mine and then go straight to the quarry and dig out the stone. A man came to him and told him that he could go to his store and take all the timber, lime and slate he required.

When it was time to employ the masons, Billy went around the west of Cornwall trying to raise the money, and when he came to St Ives he found them in a very poor way as few fish had been caught that year. Billy went up to the Wesleyan Chapel and with some powerful believers they asked the Lord to send fish. They prayed until midnight and as they left the meeting they found out that some fishermen had caught ten thousand fish and others twenty thousand. Some of the fisherman told him to get a boat and row out to where the fish were; he did so and they scooped many fish into the boat. Billy took the fish and sold them for £6.75. He went home with enough to pay the masons and the chapel was completed.

Notice how Billy did not ignore his calling because he was concerned about the time he wanted to spend with his wife and seven children; he made time. Notice also how he did not delay the work until he had the money to complete the chapel; he stepped out and the Lord equipped him with everything he needed as he needed it. Even though this happened 170 years ago we can learn a lot from Billy Bray. We all have work to do for the Lord and if we all step out, together we will change this nation.

Here are some practical ideas to help you find out your calling and 'step out'.

Discover your passions and identify your gifts

It is likely that the passions you had before you became a Christian were ones put in you by the Lord. My passion for history and my desire to network were in me long before I gave my life to the Lord and they are now the mainstays of my ministry. Discover your primary gifts and do not try to specialise in anything that involves a secondary gift because you will have a hard time; like the pastor who was not a pastor.

Make space for God to move

At the start of 2001 I decided to cut my work down to just one day a week so that I could make my time available to God. I decided that time was marching on and I did not want to miss my destiny so I said to the Lord, 'Here I am, do with me what you will.' I still did not really know the fullness of my calling at that time. I was fortunate that I could scrape by on one day a week's income plus my savings, and not many of you can take such a measure, but you can still unclutter your day and give God space to move. Going to prophetic, healing and signs and wonders conferences is also making space for God. God can meet you anywhere but sometimes if you go away for a few days, away from work, friends and the phone, God can break through.

Fast

God specifically told me to fast for 40 days when I cut my work down. Would you believe it, the one time I knew I heard God was for Him to tell me to fast. I e-mailed friends who pray for me and told them that I was sure one of them would have a word that I was mistaken, but nobody responded! I should point out to those of you who find fasting difficult that I hardly noticed that I was on my juice and water fast until the last week when I started to think about what I was going to eat at the end of it. This confirmed to me that I was doing the Lord's will. You obviously don't have to do a 40 day fast; just do what you feel the Lord is saying. After the fast I did notice that the things I was doing were accelerating and the vision became clearer.

Press in to God

This is obvious and I am not going to tell you how to do this, but clearly the more time we spend with God, reading His Word and resting in His presence, the more we will hear Him. I would also advise you to spend as much time in the atmosphere of God as you can. If the Holy Spirit is not very apparent in your church then go to where He is. I originally went to as many conferences as I could because I knew there would be a powerful anointing at these places and that some of it would rub off on me. I now go for networking purposes, but I also go when I feel dry and want to soak in His presence. The ideal, of course, is to have that atmosphere in your home; if you have that then spend time resting in His presence, listening to Him every way you know. If you have difficulty hearing God then use your contacts to find out where you can go to be activated in the prophetic gifts; there are more and more of these types of courses around these days; Sharon Stone is wonderful at this. Over the years I have had several home groups for hungry people where we have just asked the Lord to come into our midst. If you know of such a group, see if you can be invited, because it is good to be around like minded people and in the presence of God.

Holiness

There is no doubt that we are called to be set apart from all that is sinful, impure and immoral. The more pure we are the closer we get to God and the more He can use us. In the eighteenth century the Methodists were very strong in this area, however today it does not receive the same attention. The Methodists had Societies where men would gather together (or women) and they would tell one another what impure thoughts or actions they had participated in since the last meeting. I would recommend that you find a prayer partner (or two), of the same gender and be accountable to one another for your thoughts and actions. They can also help guide you and advise you. This is not easy because telling people about one's sexual thoughts etc is embarrassing but it is a good way to help us stay focused and pure. Our lives must stand up to the teachings of Jesus so that we can be used to our fullest.

Counselling

Do not be held back because someone might say you have issues to resolve in your life (unless it is something serious like an addiction); we all do, and if we waited until they were all resolved none of us would minister anywhere. If there are issues in your life, and there are bound to be, then go to people you can trust to confirm it and then go and get some counselling, but if God opens doors then go through them; He knows if you are in a position to fulfil His plans for you.

Dream big

We have a big God who has big dreams for us; remember what Pastor Victoria said, 'Our pastor teaches us to believe in the impossible'. Open your mind, go to where you can see miracles happen, keep stretching your boundaries; keep in touch with what God is doing around the world. I wanted to see in person the miracles I had read about and I wanted to do them myself, so I went on these trips to different parts of the world where I knew God was doing amazing things. The more I saw, the more I wanted to do myself and the more I did through God's grace. My faith gets built up every time I go away and I grow as a person and spiritually. Read books about the lives of Christian heroes of the past or go onto my website www.ukwells.org and read about some of them there. As I read about what they achieved I just want to emulate them or even exceed what they did; they really inspire me. I understand that I am a single man and cannot possibly understand fully the pressures on a family, but I say to the husband or wife, please consider going on one of these trips. I have friends who tell me that they just cannot manage it while their children are growing up, but God can always make a way and any short term aggravation with children will be more than compensated by your increased faith and the increased presence of the Holy Spirit in your life. If you really cannot go on one of these trips at least go to a conference, a mission in the United Kingdom or read about past great saints. Something else I come up against is, 'The Lord has not said that I can go'. Why on earth should God not want you to go somewhere when the only reason for your going is to experience more of Him and his Kingdom? Going to Africa, Brazil, Ukraine etc will stretch you and help you to dream big!

Do not be discouraged

Like Tatyana, if nothing happens immediately, press in. Write down your vision and pray it in; continually ask the Lord to water the seed that is in your heart. Be watchful and be expectant. The opportunity may come when you least expect it. Do not think that it needs to take years of preparation before you are used by God or before you step out in your calling; you will never be ready for what God is going to give you, so never say 'I am not yet equipped

172

enough'. Do not allow people to limit or discourage you; you can be used by God the day you give your life to Him; you do not have to do an Alpha course or a discipleship course first. Remember that the disciples had less than three years' teaching before they were doing miraculous things. Remember also the demoniac in Luke 8. After deliverance Jesus told him, 'Return home and tell how much God has done for you.' He was evangelising within hours of conversion. The three women from Pastor Sunday's church were all walking in their calling less than four years from coming to the Lord and their ministries exploded less than two years from them starting them.

Step out

Do not sit at home waiting for God to drop a ministry into your lap; it just does not happen that way. God likes us to be proactive, to step out in faith towards something. If we make small steps forward He will tend to open the doors. If you hear God asking you to do something then obey; it is OK to ask for confirmation but do not keep asking for confirmations, just step out. Be prepared to take a risk, I do not think that God minds us making a mistake. Look at the parable of the talents; God was angry with the man who hid his talent in the ground, He would much rather the man had taken a risk and invested the money, even if he lost it. Many years ago I was determined to step out and serve God, so I stepped out in three areas, believing that I was in the will of God. All three were a disaster, and I told God that that was the last time I was going to step out, I was just going to sit in church and go through the motions of being a Christian. Two months later I was at a friend's church and he had a visiting speaker from Argentina. Someone had told me that the visitor was the holiest man she had ever met, so I was keen to receive prayer from him. I went up after the service for prayer and through an interpreter he said just eight words over me. 'Do not fear man, be a risk taker.' It was not what I wanted to hear, but from that moment on I have tried to do what he said.

Remember what I have already mentioned a couple of times. Go to the Bible, go to the sources I have mentioned and check what I have written.

If you are in a church with a loving pastor who is envisioning you, equipping you and helping you to step out into your calling, then that is wonderful. If your church is not releasing you then go to your pastor and put your cards on the table; explain how you feel and what you require, I am sure that he will listen sympathetically. If it is clear that you are not going to be equipped and released then ask the Lord where you should be. It may be right to stay where you are and fellowship with like minded people in your church, but remember that church does not need to be inside the four walls of a building. Church is wherever there is an assembly of two or three people. We must stop thinking of church as being a building; it could be in a car park, a field or a coffee shop. Just follow the Lord's leading. Do not feel intimidated by the idea of not being in a formal church; it is quite alright if you meet with mature Christian friends who you are accountable to. Our headship is Christ. Nobody else can fulfil that role and the important thing is to be where He wants us to be and to be where we can fulfil the calling that we have from Christ. Remember, you will be held accountable for what you have done or not done.

I am not saying here that there is not a role for the gathering in a church building. Corporate worship is important and it is good to attend such meetings, but it is my belief that the important thing is that we fulfil God's plan for our lives and if we are being held back in doing this then we must ask God to show where we should be. There will always be plenty of opportunities to attend corporate worship somewhere, even if the regular gathering one attends is only made up of a few people. The overriding passion in my life is to fulfil every plan that God has for me. Wouldn't it be terrible if we got to heaven and the Lord showed us all the things we could have achieved in His name but didn't? It does not bear thinking about. I pray that for all of you the only words you will hear when your time comes, is 'Well done, good and faithful servant!'

Conclusion

There are two messages in this book; the first is that I, along with the Holy Spirit, am calling the Church to reform. I am saying that the Reformation of five hundred years ago only went part of the way, so I am calling on the Church to complete what began so long ago. Today is a new day, it is time for a new wineskin; we need to move forward from the foundation that was laid by the early Church. A few churches are there, some more are on the way there, but many are still a long way off. I am asking for the pastor to change his idea of what Church is and what his role is within it and I am asking for members of the congregation to recognise that their role is not just to go to church on Sunday. It is time for the Church to be reformed; we must get the Church back to being fit for purpose.

The second message is that I am calling the saints to rise up and take the place that God has prepared in advance for them. Today is the day of the saints, not the day of the priest, and the nation needs you to step out to fulfil your destiny in Christ. The state of this nation will not change unless we step out and influence society. In the past we had people like William Wilberforce, Lord Shaftesbury and Elizabeth Fry who stood up to make a difference. Now it is time for you to stand up; it is time for you to step out in your calling!

Bibliography

The Church and Ministry in the Early Centuries, by Thomas M Lindsay, published by Hodder and Stoughton 1903.

History of the Christian Church, Volume I, AD1-311 by Phillip Schaff, published by T&T Clark 1869.

The Church under Siege, by M A Smith, published by Inter-Varsity Press 1976.

The Rise of Christianity, by W H C Frend, published by Darton, Longman and Todd 1984.

A History of Christianity, by K S Latourette, published by Eyre and Spottiswoode 1954.

A Manual of Church History Volume 1, by A H Newman, published by The American Baptist Publication Society 1904.

Beyond Tithing, by Stuart Murray, published by Paternoster Press 2000.

A Short History of the Early Church, by H R Boer, published by William B Eerdmans Publishing Company 1976.

Pagan Christianity, by Frank Viola, published by Present Testimony Ministry 2002.

To Preach or Not to Preach, by David C. Norrington, published by Paternoster Press 1996.

The Messianic Church Arising, by Dr Robert D Heidler, published by Glory of Zion International Ministries 2006.

The Reformation in England Volume 2, by J H Merle d'Aubigne, first published in 1853 and then by The Banner of Truth Trust 1962.

Confronting the Queen of Heaven, by Peter Wagner, published by Wagner Publications 1998.

Here I Stand, Martin Luther, by Roland Bainton, published by Lion Publishing Plc 1978.

When you Can't Live and Yet You Can't Die, by Tatyana Galushko, published by Fares Publishing House.

Common Ground, by Jordan Bajis, http://www.rebuildjournal.org/ resbkexcrptfldr/commongroundchptreleven.html

Rethinking the Wineskin, by Frank Viola, published by Present Testimony Ministry 2001

Who is your Covering?, by Frank Viola, published by Present Testimony Ministry 2001

Billy Bray, the King's Son, by F W Bourne, published by Epworth Press 1937 (originally 1877)

From Death Unto Life, by William Haslam.

The Day of the Saints, by Dr Bill Hamon, published by Destiny Image Publishers Inc 2002